Flawed Pots

*Dealing with the
Challenges of Difficult
& Toxic Christians*

Dr. Donald Davenport

"Flawed Pots: Dealing with the Challenges of Difficult & Toxic Christians," by Dr. Donald Davenport. ISBN 978-1-949756-58-6 (softcover).

Published 2019 by Virtualbookworm.com Publishing Inc., P.O. Box 9949, College Station, TX 77842, US. ©2019, Donald Davenport. All rights reserved. No part of this publication may be reproduced, stored in a retrieval system, or transmitted in any form or by any means, electronic, mechanical, recording or otherwise, without the prior written permission of Donald Davenport.

Contents

Preface 1
Introduction.. 4
Chapter 1: Dealing with Difficult and Toxic
People 9
    The Story of The Flawed Pot............................ 9
    Toxic Relationships 12
    What Makes a Relationship Toxic?................ 13
    What are the Warning Signs of a Toxic
    Relationship? 14
    What Does the Bible say about Dealing with . 16
    Difficult and Toxic People?............................. 16
    Christians and Church People......................... 16
    Six Responses to Handle Insults
    as a Christian 24
    Six Strategies to Learn From King David to
    Handle Negative Comments........................... 25
Chapter 2: Gray Areas that Create Difficult People
and Difficult Situations.. 28
    Apostle Paul and Conflict in the
    Early Church... 28
    WEAK VS STRONG EXAMPLE 38
Chapter 3: Elephants in the Room 41
    Characteristics of the Types of Jezebel
    Personalities in a Church or Organization...... 43
Chapter 4: The Challenges of a Jezebel Spirit.... 46
    Jezebel and Naboth's Vineyard 50

Suggested Process of Confronting a Jezebel Spirit 52
How Does One Discern a Jezebel Spirit? 55
Jezebel's Character Traits 55
Signs that Your Ministry or Organization Has a Jezebel Spirit.. 59
Potential Toxic Leaders in Churches 60

Chapter 5: Fighting Righteously 62

Dealing with Mean and Difficult People with Empathy and Humility..................................... 77
Difficult Personality of a Spouse 78

Chapter 6: These People Can Be Frustrating 82

8 Examples of Passive Aggressive Behavior . 82
Absalom Spirit 83
12 Ways your Passive Aggressiveness is Slowly Killing your Relationships............................... 85

Chapter 7: How Do We Deal with Them 93

Our Responsibility as Believers 101

Chapter 8: Steps to Loving Unlovable People .. 103

Understanding People Through Their Personality The DISC Method 105

Chapter 9: It's Not Always What You Think ... 110

Be Careful in Your Dealings with Them 111
We Need a Mirror, Not a Window 113
Look in the Mirror Before You Look Out the Window 114
The Faithful Dog and His Master.................. 117
Conclusion 118

ADDENDUM 120

BEHAVIORAL ZONES 123

Sources and Works Cited.................................... 125

Preface

I like to give special thanks and appreciation to my wife, Frances, without whom this book would have been difficult to complete. In many ways she has taught me much through her character, temperament, and actions about how to relate and deal with all kinds and types of challenging people.

Special thanks to the congregation that I was privileged to pastor for over 21 years; it was there that I grew from all my limitations and allowed me to grow as a pastoral leader. Special appreciation to the Evangelical Covenant Church denomination in which I served on a denominational level for over 10 years. It was there that I served in my role to start and grow new churches, and to settle many of the ebb-and-flow challenges they each faced as congregations.

In my over 40 years of serving in parachurch, local congregations, and national level leadership, I have personally evolved and grown to develop a healthy understanding of the kingdom of God, and for that I am deeply appreciative.

Some brief information about Don Davenport

Donald Davenport was born in Chicago, Illinois. He sensed the call of God upon graduating from college to connect and serve through various parachurch ministries. Afterward, he served as an associate pastor of a church in Chicago.

Dr. Davenport also served as Lead Pastor of the Community Covenant Church in Calumet Park, Illinois, for over twenty-one years. He served in leadership at the national office in Chicago in the ministry of church growth in the Evangelical Covenant Church denomination for twelve years.

He is the recipient of several awards. One such example is a Proclamation by the United States Congress for Community Service in 1993, which is filed in the Library of Congress in Washington, D.C. He was awarded a street sign named in his honor by the Calumet Park Illinois city council. Dr Davenport is a member of the American Christian Counseling Association. He has served as guest professor of preaching at North Park Seminary. He has traveled, preached, and lectured throughout the United States and internationally. He received his bachelor's degree from Southern Illinois University, Garrett Seminary (graduate theological school of Northwestern University) and his doctorate in counseling from Bethany Seminary.

Dr Davenport has published two books: "7 Healthy Stages in Male and Female Relationships" and "The Intentional Leader," Both are now available online to download as a ebook or purchase in hard or soft copy through www.amazon.com. He is also in the process of completing a children's book, soon to be published.

He has written booklets and published articles such as "Transformational Urban Church Planting," "Understanding the Racial Divide in America and the Church," and many other articles.

As a pastor, he gave leadership to successfully revive a church that was near closing its doors. It is now continuing to evolve into a healthy and vibrant church ministry. He is the founder of Harvest Life, a ministry that is involved in consulting, counseling, micro-financing small businesses in various countries in Africa, peer mentoring, and cohort development of leaders.

Dr. Davenport is the husband of Frances, a former school teacher; they have been blessed with five children and live in the south suburbs in the Chicagoland area.

Introduction

My purpose for this book is not to be an exhaustive guide to solve all problems and conflicts. It is rather to help us understand and be problem-solvers and peacemakers when difficult situations or difficult persons potentially disrupt the mission and culture of an organization, group or personal relationship. Nor is this book about putting down or demeaning people who may have challenging personalities. It really is about finding ways to glean the best of us in often difficult situations and conversations. It is not easy for me to believe and confess that there are some Christian believers who would be capable of toxic behaviors. The reality is, all of us are capable of these behaviors because of our flawed natures as humans to express difficult behaviors at times. However, how we react to others just might tell us more about ourselves than it does about the person getting on our nerves. We're responsible for our own emotions and emotional responses.

All of us are in a continual state of spiritual growth and maturity. Some slower than others. Some much slower than others. Some believers mature and grow, and others sadly will never change. They have decided that their flaw is something that represents who they are, and they expect others to conform and deal with it. It is often so easy to place our spiritual heads in the sand and hope that over time, the situation or behavior will change or go away. I have often said "give them enough rope and they will eventually hang themselves." Sometimes this is true, and sometimes not.

Let me say from the beginning that it is not easy to confront difficult people in these situations. Again, it is easier to believe and hope that over time, these challenges will take care of themselves. As we all know, it never really goes away. It continually grows, festers and manifests itself into an ugly sore. This sore evolves over time like yeast, and creates and causes a mass emotional explosion of behaviors and divisions to rise within a church, group, organization, or even a family unit.

This growing hostility potentially moves from being minor to something major, such as church divisions, divisive home lives, and relationships that never fully heal. This hostility creates lingering and enduring wounds that swells and become a chronic narrative in the life of that group or relationship. Organizations, and people in general, do a poor job in working through various difficulties in their midst. *In many ways, this book can be the relationship conflict handbook for individual homes, organizations, and churches who seek understanding to work through the challenges that often confront them.* This book is also for those who have had or are having similar experiences of the toxic behaviors listed:

- Belittling, bullying and making someone feel unimportant
- Name-calling
- Being treated with disrespect
- Constant nitpicking, criticizing, flying off the handle over trivial or minor matters
- Using secrets and shame in the home as a weapon against a family member
- Making someone feel bad and ashamed
- Deliberately overloading someone with work
- Undermining someone, such as setting them up to fail
- Purposefully withholding information which is needed for the person to do their work efficiently
- Excluding or isolating someone from normal workplace or ministry conversation
- Making someone feel unwelcome
- Shouting at someone, whether in private or public in front of people
- Creating cliques that foster exclusion and alienation
- Spreading rumors that are partially or fully untrue
- Creating a problem in a congregation, workplace or ministry and claiming someone else caused it, not taking responsibility, and saying "it's not my fault"
- Refusing to leave a position in the organization or ministry creating tension in the environment
- Constant micro-managing of coworkers, team members, or leadership.

- People who are over-sensitive to the point that others have to walk on eggshells in order to co-exist with this person
- Isolating someone from their friends and family in order to create or maintain abusive behavior
- Constantly blaming and condemning your spouse or friend in order to have an excuse to continue abusive behavior, such as physically and verbally harming them.
- Using their wealth of resources, such as money, influence, and connections, to maintain control over a group or organization.

Review these behaviors again. Ask yourself if, in your various social relationships, you have encountered anyone who exhibits these behaviors. If you are really honest with yourself, ask if you have ever been guilty of demonstrating any of the behaviors listed. Maybe you need some tools, guidelines, and boundaries that will assist you with being a problem-solver in times of difficulty. Christian churches and organizations may want to see this book as a handbook for their ministries to assist as a guide in settling and managing conflicts, etc. If any of these areas connect your personal dots, this book may be for you. This book will also attempt to briefly explore some of these challenges in the secular, congregational, and Christian life relationships in general.

The Bible tells us that all of us are made from God's divine hands, and we all have defective human emotional parts that need to be understood for what they are, and each of us needs to be given a second chance for grace and redemption.

Flawed Pots

There is a song from the popular hip-hop artist Beyonce's CD called "Flaws and All". She sings a verse that reveals the complexity often residing in many of us:

"I'm a train wreck in the morning
I'm a bitch in the afternoon
Every now and then without warning
I can be really mean towards you
I'm a puzzle, yes, indeed
Ever-complex in every way
And all the pieces aren't even in the box
And yet you see the picture clear as day"

And the vessel that He made of clay was marred in the hand of the potter, so he made it again another vessel as seemed good-to the potter to make it. Jeremiah 18.4 KJV

Yes, all of us with our flaws, and all are *beautifully broken.*

Chapter 1:
Dealing with Difficult and Toxic People

What you allow is what will continue, and what you ignore, you empower.

Let's be honest: each of us have our emotional, social, character, personality, and spiritual flaw(s) that could potentially cause us to be difficult people. As a result, we often find ourselves either consciously or unconsciously creating disharmony and conflict in our homes, places of employment, and yes, even in the Body of Christ. However, we never know what God in His divine providence can do with our flaws and the flaws of others. God has made each of us "Perfectly Flaw some". Here is a story of such.

The Story of The Flawed Pot
There is a story of a man who carried water in India who had two large pots, each hung on opposite ends of a pole which he carried across his neck. One

Flawed Pots

of the pots had a crack in it, and while the other pot was perfect and always delivered a full portion of water at the end of the long walk from the stream to the master's house, the cracked pot arrived only half full. For a full two years, this went on daily, with the water carrier delivering only one and a half pots full of water to his master's house.

Of course, the perfect pot was proud of its accomplishments, perfect to the end for which it was made. But the poor cracked pot was ashamed of its own imperfection, and miserable that it was able to accomplish only half of what it had been made to do. After two years of what it perceived to be a bitter failure, it spoke to the water-bearer one day by the stream. "I am ashamed of myself, and I want to apologize to you. "Why?" asked the bearer. "What are you ashamed of?" "I have been able, for these past two years, to deliver only half my load because this crack in my side causes water to leak out all the way back to your master's house. Because of my flaws, you have to do all of this work, and you don't get full value from your efforts," the pot said. The water carrier felt sorry for the old cracked pot, and in his compassion, he said, "As we return to the master's house, I want you to notice the beautiful flowers along the path."

Indeed, as they went up the hill, the old cracked pot took notice of the sun warming the beautiful wild flowers on the side of the path, and this cheered it some. But at the end of the trail, it still felt bad because it had leaked out half its load, and so again the pot apologized to the bearer for its failure.

Dr. Donald Davenport

The water carrier said to the pot, "Did you notice that there were flowers only on your side of your path, but not on the other pot's side? That's because I have always known about your flaw, and I took advantage of it. I planted flower seeds on your side of the path, and every day while we walk back from the stream, you've watered them. For two years I have been able to pick these beautiful flowers to decorate my master's table. Without you and the flaw in the pot, he would not have this beauty to grace his house."

Each of us has our own unique flaws. Essentially, we are all by our sinful nature cracked and flawed pots. But if we are honest with ourselves and seek to grow, the Lord will use our flaws and others to grace His Father's table. In God's great purpose and plan, nothing goes to waste. Don't be afraid of your flaws and our differences with others. Acknowledge them and grow to live in peace with those who may view the world through the lens of their faith differently. Maybe you too can be the cause of beauty. Know that in our weaknesses, we find our common strength to pursue possibly a common purpose.

The Apostle Paul gives us an enduring principle: *"Whatever you do, whether in word or deed, do it all in the name of the Lord Jesus, giving thanks to God the father through him." Colossians 3:17*

Let me confess, first of all, that I love the ministries and the organizations that I worked for over the years. The only problem is the people, and in particular, the cracked and flawed pots of difficult personalities. If I didn't have to work with people, life would been wonderful! Of course, this isn't reasonable and is meant to be humorous, just in case you thought I was serious.

As Christians the new reality is, we should strive to get along with all the people that we work, worship, and yes, even live with. Sometimes God wants to use their flaws to force us to look at corrections and flaws in our own hearts. That does not mean we have to always agree with them, but we also should not intentionally look for opportunities to anger and alienate people away from God.

Romans 12:18 tells us, "If it be possible, as much as lies in you, live peaceably with all men." This verse does not say it will always be possible, but we should try.

"Brothers and sisters, if someone is caught in a sin, you who live by the Spirit should restore that person gently. But watch yourselves, or you also may be tempted. Carry each other's burdens, and in this way you will fulfill the law of Christ." Galatians 6:1-2 NIV

Toxic Relationships

Here's what you need to know in general about toxic relationships, and how to tell if you're in a toxic or difficult situation.

Dr. Lillian Glass, a California-based communication and psychology expert who says she coined the term in her 1995 book *Toxic People*, defines a toxic relationship as *"any relationship between people who don't support each other, where there's conflict and one seeks to undermine the other, where there's competition, where there's disrespect and a lack of cohesiveness."*

While every relationship goes through ups and downs, Glass says a toxic relationship is consistently unpleasant and draining for the people in it, to the point that negative moments outweigh and outnumber the positive ones. Dr. Kristen Fuller, a California-based family medicine physician who specializes in mental health, adds that toxic relationships are mentally, emotionally, and possibly even physically damaging to one or both people. And these relationships don't have to be romantic: Glass says friendly, familial, and professional relationships can all be toxic as well.

What makes a relationship toxic?

Fuller says people who consistently undermine or cause harm to a partner or co-worker — whether intentionally or not — often have a reason for their behavior, even if it's subconscious. "Maybe they were in a toxic relationship, either romantically or as a child. Maybe they didn't have the most supportive, loving upbringing. Fuller further says, "They could have been bullied in school. They could be suffering from an undiagnosed mental health disorder, such as depression or anxiety or bipolar disorder, an eating disorder, any form of trauma."

That was the case for Carolyn Gamble, a 57-year-old, Maryland-based motivational speaker who says she fell into toxic relationships after a difficult childhood marked by losing her mother to a drug overdose and suffering physical abuse at the hands of her father. When she grew up, she found some of the same themes in her marriage to her now-ex-husband, who she says became verbally and emotionally abusive. "I realized in this life, regardless of the cards that we're dealt, sometimes there are things that we have to let go," she says. Sometimes, Glass says, toxic relationships are simply the result of an imperfect pairing — like two people who both need control, or a sarcastic type dating someone with thin skin. "It's just that the combination is wrong," she says. There is a woman named Heidi Brocke, a 46-year-old chiropractor living in Illinois, who is familiar with these mismatches. Brocke considers herself a people-pleaser and grew up "assuming everybody was nice and everybody wanted what was best for you." Instead, she says her personality attracted controlling partners who forced her to sacrifice her needs for theirs, and to constantly work for approval that never came.

Though they had very different stories, both Brocke and Gamble say they endured toxic relationships for years — reminding us that no two bad relationships are exactly alike.

What are the warning signs of a toxic relationship?

The most serious warning signs include any form of violence, abuse, or harassment, which should be dealt with immediately. But in many cases, the indicators of a toxic relationship are much more subtle. Yes, this abuse and violence can take place in Christian and non-Christian homes alike.

The first, and simplest, is persistent unhappiness, Glass says. If a relationship stops bringing joy, and instead consistently makes you feel sad, angry, anxious, or "resigned, like you've sold out," it may be toxic, Glass says. You may also find yourself envious of happy couples.

Fuller says negative shifts in your mental health, personality, or self-esteem are all red flags, too. These changes could range from clinically diagnosable conditions, such as depression, anxiety, or eating disorders, to constantly feeling nervous or uncomfortable especially around your partner. Feeling like you can't talk with or voice concerns to your significant other is another sign that something is amiss, Fuller says.

You should also look out for changes in your other relationships, or in the ways you spend your free time, Fuller says. "You may feel bad for doing things on your own time, because you feel like you have to attend to your partner all the time," she says. "You cross the line when you're not your individual self anymore and you're giving everything to your partner."

Finally, Fuller says, concern from family or friends should be taken seriously, particularly since people in toxic relationships are often the last to realize it. Brocke says that was true of her relationships, which perpetuated the damage for years.

"By the time I actually started realizing I was in something that wasn't healthy, it was so normal to me that it didn't seem like that big a deal," Brocke says. "You get paralyzed in it, because you're just used to it." The danger in toxic situations is that it becomes the new normal, and we settle for learning to just deal with it and it becomes no big deal. We will say, "Well, that's just the way he or she is." Many times people will say about themselves that "it's just who I am" or "you just have to accept me." Do you know people like this? Well, this book may be just for you.

What does the Bible say about dealing with difficult and toxic people?

Christians and Church People

I usually don't have any problems with Christians; it's usually the church people that I struggle with, and to be honest with you, I would sometimes rather not be around them. The Bible tells us about some church people that Jesus struggled with as well. They were the Sanhedrin Council. It consisted mainly of men who were called pharisees and sadducees. They were religious leaders who governed the laws of people and who were essentially the gatekeepers of the church. This council was initially formed hundreds of years earlier in the time of Moses, because Moses became burdened with the responsibilities of leading these Jewish refugees from four hundred years of enslavement from Egypt. Moses' father-in-law, Jethro, counseled him to choose seventy faithful men to assist him to counsel and lead these people. Over time these men, who were chosen to be helpers, have now evolved and splintered into men hardened in their religious positions by the time of Christ. These same people who were chosen to ease the burden of Moses are now the same people, generations later, who became toxic burdens and facilitated the death of our savior. Jesus had many struggles with these men, who believed that they could impress others with their religious and ostentatious clothing that gave others the impression that they were spiritually elevated above others.

Jesus goes in to say.....Woe to you Pharisees, because you love the front seats in the synagogues and the greetings in the marketplace. Woe to you because you are as graves that are clearly visible that men walk on it and do not know it. Woe to you, because you are as those graves* that are not clearly visible that men walk on and do not know it!" Luke 11.43,44

Jesus uses the word 'woe' three times in this passage. What does this mean? It is used to express grief, regret, or distress. This is a condition of deep suffering from misfortune, affliction, or grief. It is easily understood for Jesus to mean that God is very disappointed that they were created.

Essentially, too many church people are similar to these Sanhedrin factions. They have a form of Christianity, but are empty and heartless on the inside. They go to church, but Christ is not in them. They often are in key positions and organizations in the ministry, but often create ministry roadblocks because of their legalistic and heartless positions in how they understand God. As a result, they can become difficult and toxic in their relationships. Many of them may be good people but often blinded by their biases, weaknesses, flaws, and prejudices. Here are only some of their characteristics below:

a. Cause of constant dissensions and frustrations in the ministry
b. They give financially out of obligation, rather than from the heart
c. They see the church as a way to promote their products, gain status in the community, enrich their pockets.
d. They see the church not as a ministry to expand God's influence, but rather as a country or social club.
e. They view the church as a business only, rather than as a community of people to bring healing and support for each other.
f. They use the church as a place to prey on unsuspecting people for favors, abuses of various kinds, sexual dalliances, and the list goes on.
g. They will find themselves in clusters of cliques, complaining and spreading rumors that assail the integrity of the ministry.
h. They are never satisfied with the leadership, particularly with the pastoral leaders.
i. Lastly, they rarely outwardly smile; if they do smile, they are frowning on the inside.

Difficult people are everywhere. Hostile, rude, mean, selfish, impatient, uncaring, and worse (1Corinthians 6:9-11). What may be shocking to many of us is that we have and can act the same as these people. Are we always hostile, rude, mean, selfish, impatient, and uncaring? No, but we all have the seeds of all these attitudes in our hearts (Matthew 15:19; Jeremiah 17:9). Therefore, the first step in helping us deal with difficult people is understanding that we are not better than these people by nature (Ephesians 2:1–3). We live in a fallen world filled with sinful people. We must remind ourselves of this fact, so that we are not surprised when we encounter difficult people, or when we find ourselves being difficult people.

If we have received Jesus Christ, then we are forgiven for these sinful attitudes and behaviors. When we find ourselves displaying such attitudes and behaviors, we confess to God and trust that He has already forgiven us and will cleanse us (1 John 1:8–9). We make amends when possible and seek to live differently. God's forgiveness of our difficulties/sinfulness is the basis for how we are to respond to difficult people, which is with grace.

As believers in Christ, our mandate is not to get even or return evil for evil, but to return evil with good (Romans 12:19–21). We are called to love our enemies and to pray for those who persecute us (Matthew 5:43–45). This may seem impossible, and in our own power, it is impossible. However, with God working in us, it is possible (Matthew 19:26).

To return evil with good may make us feel good about our sense of justice, and sometimes rightly so. However, we must remember that it is God's role to give out justice. We are to leave the matter in God's hands and trust that He will judge justly (Romans 12:19). Most importantly, we must realize that we have not received what we deserve from God, but have received mercy and unmerited favor instead. While we were hostile and at enmity with

God, He sent His Son to die for our sins (Romans 5:6–8). Jesus, even while He was being persecuted, prayed for His tormentors (Luke 23:34).

As a point of clarity, it is not wrong to involve legal authorities. Criminal behavior is not what we are referring to when we talk about "difficult people." Social authorities have been put in place by God to uphold the law, and it is not wrong to use them (Romans 13:1–7). However, we are not to seek societal justice out of vengeance. Similarly, depending on the difficult behavior, it is not wrong to involve church authorities. Matthew 18:15–20 outlines the proper procedure for addressing grievances among church members. Again, the intent is not to seek vengeance, but to bring about peace.

As believers in Christ, we are in-dwelt by the Spirit of God, who produces the attitudes of love, joy, peace, long-suffering (patience, forbearance), kindness, goodness, faithfulness, gentleness, and self-control (Galatians 5:22–23). Therefore, we are to continually and daily pray to be filled with the Spirit, and to keep in step with the Spirit, and not grieve Him (Ephesians 4:30; 5:18). If we are to respond to difficult people with grace and love, we must depend upon and draw upon the power of God's Spirit. When we become angry and return evil with evil, we must quickly confess our fault and ask God for the grace to imitate Jesus Christ and show ourselves to be sons and daughters of our merciful Father (Luke 6:36).

If we refuse to love our enemies, then we are imitating not our Heavenly Father, but the unforgiving servant (Matthew 18:21–35). It is in our eternal best interests to imitate the former and not the latter. How can we who have received such grace and forgiveness from God refuse to show the same to others?

Often it is simple to know how we *should* act toward difficult people, but it can be quite a challenge to do so in our daily lives. The scripture in Proverbs have some excellent practical advice. For example, Proverbs 15:1 says, *"A soft answer turns away wrath, but a harsh word stirs up anger."* We can memorize this verse and, when confronted by a difficult person, attempt to respond with gentleness. You might be surprised how the situation de-escalates.

Proverbs 12:16 says:
"The vexation of a fool is known at once, but the prudent ignores an insult."

Rather than take insults personally and respond with immediate offense, we can learn to simply ignore them. Proverbs 20:3 says, *"It is an honor for a man to keep aloof from strife, but every fool will be quarreling."*

Titus 3:9 has similar encouragement to *"avoid foolish controversies, genealogies, dissensions, and quarrels about the law, for they are unprofitable and worthless."*

Proverbs 17:14 *similarly encourages ending quarrels before they begin. We can remind ourselves of the things that really matter and remember that some quarrels are simply pointless. There is no use getting entangled with a difficult person when the end result is "unprofitable and worthless."*

In some situations, it is best to try to avoid certain difficult people altogether. Proverbs 22:24–25 says, "*Make no friendship with a man given to anger, nor go with a wrathful man, lest you learn his ways and entangle yourself in a snare.*"

First Corinthians 15:33 says, "*Do not be deceived: 'Bad company ruins good morals.'*"

As much as we are able, we should make friendships with those who are seeking to honor God the same way we are. We are also called to live peaceably with others as far as we are able (Romans 12:18).

We can be proactive in dealing with difficult people by reading and even memorizing God's Word to give us the right perspective on life. His Word tells us that all people are made in His image (Genesis 1:26). When we view others as image-bearers, we may find it easier to bear with them. We can also recognize that dealing with difficult people is a trial and a tool that God can use to produce and shape good things in us.

Dealing with difficult people becomes easier when we seek to create empathy for others. We know that we ourselves can be difficult, particularly when tired or stressed or hungry. How would we want to be treated in such situations? Matthew 7:12 talks about doing unto others as we want them to do unto us. James 2:8 talks about loving others as we love ourselves.

First Peter 4:8 says, *"Above all, keep loving one another earnestly, since love covers a multitude of sins"*

As we proactively seek to love one another, we will be more able to forgive offenses and deal with difficulties in a way that honors God.

Difficult people are often difficult as a result of their own internal and emotional pain. Seeing difficult people as those who are hurting and in need of Christ's touch can encourage us to forgive them. We can also pray for their healing. Perhaps in showing them kindness, as difficult as this can be, their hearts will be softened to Christ.

At times we will need to confront a difficult person or point out challenging inter-personal behaviors. This will hopefully help them stop inflicting damage on others around them, as well as aid them in their own spiritual growth. Christians are called to speak truth in love (Ephesians 4:15). This means that we speak truth because we love, and we also do so from a heart of love. Truth can sometimes be hard to share and hard to receive, but we speak it with grace out of love for others. If the difficult person in our life is an unbeliever, we share the truth of the gospel with them as well.

Dealing with difficult people requires prayer and the power of God. When we know we are going to encounter a difficult person, we should pray beforehand. Ask for God's wisdom and His strength to respond well. Remember, we can't always control what happens to us, but we can control our response to life's situations. So we can and should pray for the person, and for God's work in their life. Remind yourself of some of the biblical truths shared here. Then seek to love them as best as you can. Take any frustrations or emotional pain from your interaction with the difficult person straight to God and seek His healing and release it to God's hands. In the meantime, we can still love them at and from a distance.

Six Responses to Handle Insults as a Christian

One pastor, early on in his ministry, encountered a church member who thought he could say whatever he thought about him as the pastor. One day in a church meeting, this member spoke up and said something very demeaning.

He was shocked. Ironically, his wife was extremely sensitive and would get offended at the slightest issues. Stunned and not knowing what to do, he let it slide. But in retrospect, he said, I am convinced that it would have been better to have addressed the unkind words. By not doing so, the member got the wrong message—that his behavior was acceptable.

It's not that he was above criticism. The problem was the place and the tone in which he would have expressed his displeasure. We can't control what others will say, but we can learn and control how we should respond.

King David also had to learn to deal with negative comments.

2 Samuel 16:5-7 says: "As King David came to Bahurim, a man came out of the village cursing them. It was Shimei son of Gera, from the same clan as Saul's family. He threw stones at the king and the king's officers and all the mighty warriors who surrounded him. 'Get out of here, you murderer, you scoundrel!' he shouted at David."

Six Strategies to Learn From King David to Handle Negative Comments

1. Bear the Insults and Refuse to Retaliate

"And David said to Abishai and to all his servants, 'Look, my own son seeks my life; how much more now may this Benjaminite! Leave him alone.'" (2 Samuel 16:11a)

Like David, we should:
a. Keep our cool. (Proverbs 15:1)
b. Turn the other cheek. (Matthew 5:39)
c. Refuse revenge. (Romans 12:19)

2. Take Some Time to Consider Three Questions

Ask yourself:
a. Are these constructive or destructive comments?
b. How would God want me to respond?
c. What can I learn from this experience?

3. Respond Properly to Unkind Words

a. Remember: "A gentle answer turns away rage, but a harsh word stirs up anger." (Proverbs 15:1)

b. Plan to speak to the person in private.
c. Don't gossip about them.
d. Thank them and request that they share future concerns with you privately. Make them aware of your feelings and perspective. If there is no common ground, amicably agree to disagree. Forgive them, even if they don't deserve it, request it or receive it.

4. Remember God Is in Control

David said, "And let him curse, for the Lord has told him to."
(2 Samuel 16:11b)

David had confidence that God was still in control, and even Shimei's cursing was under God's prompting and control.

Through insults, God may be:
a. Directing us.
b. Teaching us.
c. Correcting us.

It is tempting to forget that God is sovereign when we are insulted. But He is still on His throne and working all things together for good (Romans 8:28).

5. Live for an Audience of One

We may be offended because our self-esteem is based on admiration from others. But living to please people is a waste of time: Everyone has their own opinion. Some people are never happy. Our focus should be on pleasing God, not people.

"What I want is God's approval! Am I trying to be popular with people? If I were still trying to do so, I would not be a servant of Christ." (Galatians 1:10 GNB)

6. Trust God for Restoration

David said: *"It may be that the Lord will look on the wrong done to me and that the Lord will repay me with good for his cursing today." (2 Samuel 16:12)*

David responded correctly and trusted God to reward him someday. God is always able to repair the harm that has been done. We must pray, wait, trust, and watch for the Lord to work.

There is an African saying that illustrates how difficult and toxic persons can harm others:

The Axe Forgets What the Tree Remembers

Chapter 2:
Gray Areas That Create Difficult People and Difficult Situations

If you avoid conflict to keep the peace, you will eventually start a war within yourself.

Apostle Paul and Conflict in the Early Church

"Accept the one whose faith is weak, without quarreling over disputable matters. One person's faith allows them to eat anything, but another, whose faith is weak, eats only vegetables. The one who eats everything must not treat with contempt the one who does not, and the one who does not eat everything must not judge the one who does, for God has accepted them. Who are you to judge someone else's servant? To their own master, servants stand or fall. And they will stand, for the Lord is able to make them stand. One person considers one day more sacred than another;

Dr. Donald Davenport

another considers every day alike. Each of them should be fully convinced in their own mind. Whoever regards one day as special does so to the Lord. Whoever eats meat does so to the Lord, for they give thanks to God; and whoever abstains does so to the Lord and gives thanks to God. For none of us lives for ourselves alone, and none of us dies for ourselves alone. If we live, we live for the Lord; and if we die, we die for the Lord.

So, whether we live or die, we belong to the Lord. For this very reason, Christ died and returned to life so that he might be the Lord of both the dead and the living. You, then, why do you judge your brother or sister? Or why do you treat them with contempt? For we will all stand before God's judgment seat. It is written: "'As surely as I live,' says the Lord, 'every knee will bow before me; every tongue will acknowledge God.'" So then, each of us will give an account of ourselves to God. Therefore let us stop passing judgment on one another. Instead, make up your mind not to put any stumbling block or obstacle in the way of a brother or sister. I am convinced, being fully persuaded in the Lord Jesus, that nothing is unclean in itself. But if anyone regards something as unclean, then for that person it is unclean."
Romans 14:1-14 NIV

Difficult people in the Christian family are often created and nurtured essentially because of how each of us view *similar issues differently.* There are some issues of our faith that are not clearly black or white, but lie in the gray and sometimes unclear rights or wrongs of our faith. Many of these issues over our church history have literally created and formed major divisions in the form of various denominations, divided or split churches, and various splinter Christian and religious associations. Whether it is how we see the issue of faith versus works, or how the Holy Spirit operates in the life of a believer, the purposes of the church in the world, the nature of salvation in the life of a believer, how one performs baptism or communion, our political views, or which day of the week we should worship. We can go on and on, but the question for us now should be: how should we bring peace to the body of Christ, in light of how we see and view life according to our faith differently? How can we live with our gray area differences without becoming difficult? The Bible tells us: *"If possible as much as lies within you to be at peace with one another." Romans 12:18*

In Romans 14, the apostle Paul is dealing with matters of Christian conscience and personal convictions, especially as they relate to the *strong* and *weak* Christians. Paul does not praise the conscience of the weak, nor does he condemn it. One Christian author once said that the favorite indoor sport of too many Christians is trying to change each other. In Romans chapter 14, Paul tells us not to change other people to suit our preferences, but rather to change our own conduct so as to not offend the weaker brother.

Let us first look briefly at the biblical and historical background and issues surrounding Romans 14, and the theme remains the same as in chapters 12 and 13: love your neighbor as you love yourself. But the specific issue in this chapter is how a church or family can hold itself together when some members are so different from each other.

Here, I will give a brief background into behaviors of the Jewish Christian people that will be for some reading this to be too mind-consuming. Just stay with me here. For example, there were some Jewish Christians who believed the newly converted Greek Christians should not eat meat, because it was against Jewish customs. These same Jewish Christians felt the new Greek Christians should be circumcised in order to be righteous. But the newly converted Greeks did not have any problems with it and felt that it should not be a problem. So we had the Jewish Christians judging or condemning these newly converted Christians, and the new Greek Christians judging the Jewish Christians for being so legalistic. Paul tells them they are both wrong. In other words, Paul is trying to instruct the Jews to not confuse their Christian faith with their traditional Jewish culture. Our culture doesn't save us; it merely shapes our identity. Don't use your culture as a measuring stick for how holy or righteous you are. In the same way, he reminds the new believers, don't look down on the Jewish Christians for their culture and how they were raised. Paul sums up that difference by saying that some have *weak* faith and some have *strong* faith.

You see the reference to this difference in verse 1: "As for the one who is weak in faith, welcome him, but not to quarrel over opinions." And then you see it again in Romans 15:1: "We who are strong have an obligation to bear with the failings of the weak." And then you see another parallel between the beginning of chapter 14 and the beginning of chapter 15. You see the command to "welcome" each other in Romans 14:1 ("As for the one who is weak in faith, welcome him"); and you see it again in Romans 15:7 ("Therefore welcome one another as Christ has welcomed you, for the glory of God"). So the entire chapter, plus part of chapter 15 (up through verse 13), is dealing with the danger of divisions in the church that can happen because of the differences between the weak and the strong.

So it's important that we understand what it means to be weak or strong. It's probably not exactly what you think it is. At least, I am surprised by some of what I see there. So let's start by asking what it means to be weak in faith versus strong in faith. How we should treat each other when we have these differences. Then we will look at the foundations Paul gives for this kind of loving treatment.

1. What Does It Mean to Be Weak in Faith?

Notice first that those who are weak in faith don't eat meat and don't drink wine. Verse 2: "One person believes he may eat anything, while the weak person eats only vegetables." The issue here is meat, as you can see in verse 21 where wine is added to the list: "It is good not to eat meat or drink wine, or do anything that causes your brother to stumble." So Paul is saying to the strong in faith: there are times when you deny yourself meat and wine for the sake of the weak who don't eat meat or drink wine. So that's the first thing we see about the weak and the strong. The weak avoid meat and

Dr. Donald Davenport

wine, and the strong are free to eat and drink anything.

Second, the avoidance of meat and wine—the practice of the weak—is not sin, but is God-conscious behavior. The first evidence for this is that verse 1 says they are acting in "weak faith," not no-faith. The practices of the weak are faith-driven practices. Paul says in verse 23b, "Whatever does not proceed from faith is sin." But he does not accuse the weak of sinning. They are acting from faith. Weak faith. And faith is a God-centered frame of heart.

The other evidence that the abstinence of the weak is God-conscious behavior is found in verse 6: "The one who observes the day, observes it in honor of the Lord. The one who eats, eats in honor of the Lord, since he gives thanks to God, while the one who abstains, abstains in honor of the Lord and gives thanks to God." Notice how much credit Paul gives to the weak brother who will not eat meat or drink wine. "The one who abstains, abstains in honor of the Lord and gives thanks to God. His behavior is God-directed (to the end) and he feels deeply thankful, not resentful, as he abstains. So this weak brother is acting on faith, and he is God-centered, and he is overflowing with thanks to God. Is this what you think of when you think of weak?

The third thing to say about the weak brother's abstinence from meat and wine is that it is not because he believes this behavior is the way he gets justified, or the way he secures his acceptance with God. This weak brother is not like the Judaizers in Galatia who thought that circumcision was essential to securing acceptance with God (Galatians 5:1-3). We know this because Paul was furious with this false gospel in Galatians (Galatians 1:6-9), but he gives no criticism of these weak brothers like that. They are not legalists. They do not think their abstinence earns God's acceptance or contributes to their justification.

One more thing we see in this abstinence of the weak from meat and wine, namely, is that they regard meat and wine in some sense as "unclean" or "common." Verse 14: "I know and am persuaded in the Lord Jesus that nothing is unclean in itself, but it is unclean (koinon) for anyone who thinks it unclean (koinon)." Paul wouldn't have said this if it were irrelevant to the situation. This was the view of the weak: meat and wine are in some sense "unclean."

2. Why Does Paul Call Them Weak?

So the question now is: What's weak about this abstinence from meat and wine? Why does Paul call it weak? It's based on faith. It's God-conscious. It's expressing gratitude to God, not self-sufficiency. It's not legalistic. So how is it weak? And I hope you are asking: am I in the weak category or the strong category? Or maybe I don't qualify for either. And I hope you are feeling that Paul is pretty impressed with the weak. He's thankful for them. He is practicing what he is preaching. Welcome the weak (v. 1). Don't despise the weak (v. 3).

So what is their weakness? I think the answer is the same as the answer to the question as to why they view meat and wine as "unclean." If we could understand that, I think we would see why Paul calls them weak. My answer to this question is this: The weak regard meat and wine as unclean because they believe eating meat and drinking wine will not glorify God as much as abstaining will. There is something about meat and wine that makes eating it and drinking it less honoring to God than abstaining.

I base this on the end of verse 6, where it says that "the one who abstains, abstains in honor of the Lord and gives thanks to God." In other words, the weak man is making his choices rightly on the basis of what he believes will most honor the Lord and express thanks to the Lord. They are good, well-motivated choices, given his convictions about meat and wine. He must believe that those who eat meat and drink wine don't honor the Lord as much as they would if they abstained. Why they believed this about the meat and wine, Paul doesn't say explicitly.

What's crucial to know is that Paul surely thought they were wrong in this conviction. The conviction that there is something about meat and wine that makes abstinence more honoring to God than eating and drinking was a mistake. They lacked the knowledge that would undergird and liberate their faith. They could not trust God for the joy of eating meat or drinking wine, because they lacked some crucial knowledge. They knew God, they loved God, they trusted God. But they did not understand something that would have strengthened their faith in these particular ways.

3. How Should We Practically Treat Each Other When We Have These Differences?

He says it positively in verse 1 and negatively in verse 3. Verse 1: *"As for the one who is weak in faith, welcome him, but not to quarrel over opinions."* In other words, be accepting of the weaker brother, and be sure that as you fold him into your life, you keep "divisive questionings" to a minimum. I take that to mean: questionings about meat and wine and days, etc. So the first, positive instruction Paul gives about how the strong and weak should treat each other is: welcome each other, accept each other. And don't let "divisive questionings" over non-essentials create barriers.

The negative way of saying it is in verse 3: *"Let not the one who eats despise the one who abstains, and let not the one who abstains pass judgment on the one who eats."*

Typically the strong will be tempted to "despise" the weak or look down on them. Paul has not done that in this chapter, and we should not do it either. And typically the weak will be tempted to judge the strong because, to the weak who are careful to abstain from things, the strong seem to be spiritually careless. So the weak are tempted to point out careless behavior that may well be leading to a fall—to spiritual destruction. In other words, they are not legalists who say you can't be saved if you do that; but they do say: If you are spiritually careless like that, you may drift away and be lost.

Dr. Donald Davenport

So Paul says, don't despise each other and don't judge or condemn each other, and don't build your relationships on "divisive questionings" or "quarrels over opinions." Rather, accept each other and build your lives, your relationships, on something far greater than convictions about meat and wine and days. On what? That is what Paul takes up in verses 3b and 4.

He mentions three truths that give a firm foundation for accepting each other with our differences. Verse 3b: "God has welcomed him." The strong and weak should welcome each other because God has welcomed us. Paul says again in Romans 15:7: "Welcome one another as Christ has welcomed you, for the glory of God." The great foundation for our tolerance of one another is that God has accepted us in Jesus Christ. The weak and the strong believe in Christ who died for them. They are accepted by God in Christ. We should accept them with all their differences.

As believers, we are clear in the black-and-white areas of our faith. For example, the Ten Commandments are clear. The beatitudes in the gospel are clear. We can go on and on. We become difficult in our relationships, similar to the early church (weak and strong), when we fail to resolve how we deal with each other in the gray areas of our faith. These are issues that the Bible is not clear about or has not mandated against it. Much of this is cultural, or the kind of society one was born or raised in. Whether this is whether women should wear pants or wear jewelry to church; having communion weekly, monthly or annually; whether musical instruments shall be played; the role of social activism in church in terms of whether it should be preached or taught; beliefs on pro-life or pro-choice; should someone who is divorced be in leadership; can Christians dance or dance in the sanctuary; chewing gum in the sanctuary, when is someone saved; can Christians drink alcohol; can Christians play cards; or the type and kind of music that can be played in church. I remember there was one Christian daily radio ministry that wouldn't air any songs that included drums on their radio station, for example.

WEAK VS STRONG EXAMPLE
The church decided to go to a full worship music ministry. A set of drums was placed upon the stage or pulpit area. The music selections went from completely hymn-based and soundtracks to a live worship band. Many families joined the church because of the new music ministry.

Several long-standing couples came to you expressing their concern about the stage and music. They expressed that they felt the place of worship was being turned to a rock stage or rhythm and blues sound. Their primary concern was the drums. You speak to the couples, and they leave with no satisfaction. They go out into the church and begin discussing their concerns, which makes even more people upset over the drums and the music. The question should be: how should this church resolve this matter? How do we deal with, as the early church, the weak and strong brother in this case? How can we begin the process of living in a judgment-free zone? We can begin with the basic principle of don't throw out what you don't want thrown back at you. The Bible tells us in Proverbs 26:27:

"Whoever digs a pit will fall into it; if someone rolls a stone, it will roll back on them."

What is the basic difference between judging someone and observation of their behavior?

Judging someone is essentially condemnation without clarity or understanding. In other words, creating conclusions about a matter without all of the facts, and not hearing from the heart and mind of the other person.

Observation is merely describing what we see, not blindly demonizing or forming condemning conclusions. It is seeing what it sees, filtering it through our own spiritual lens and determining based on Galatians 6:1-2 how to proceed based on what we observed.

I have found that there are three principles about judging others

1. Be careful and give it time. 1Corinthians 4.5
2. It is not always what it looks like.
3. Before you speak to them, ask yourself three questions:
   Is it true? Is it necessary? Is it kind?

Here is another example from a social network post of a Christian believer who became convicted by her own past behavior that caused an offense and difficulty toward others.

Flawed Pots

"I'm convicted. I took a mental whooping last night at my monthly group bible study which I love. Our lesson last night let me know within my heart that I've made some posts that I shouldn't have. I vacillated if I should post this but I tell almost everything else...so why stop now. We touched on several scenarios where LOVE trumps Knowledge. Sometimes you can be right but still be wrong."

"How have my post or posts impacted someone else that may have been the subject of my post? Did I build them up, or was I being opinionated (as usual) and didn't care how the opinion landed because I was "right". Have they been loving, helpful, or do they build up the body of Christ...well I know my posts don't hit on all those cylinders & have not been designed to. I have deleted some recent posts that took digs at a certain celebrity or two in my Face Book rants. I'm going to stay in my lane & post about what I normally post about..my daily musings & antics-my family-my talking dogs-life lessons-health-food-sprinkled w/ an occasional commentary on a local or world events-all told in my own "special" way-Dang that sounds boring (delete me now)-anyway I'm a work in progress. Forgive me if I've offended you. Be blessed & be a blessing"

Indeed, we sensed that she eventually recognized her weakness and was convicted of her behavior, and she confessed it openly. Yes, we all are a work in progress.

Chapter 3:
Elephants in The Room

The jungle is stronger than the elephant
African Proverb

When an ostrich senses danger and cannot run away, it flops to the ground and remains still, with its head and neck flat on the ground in front of it. Because the head and neck are lightly colored, they blend in with the color of the soil. From a distance, it just looks like the ostrich has buried its head in the sand, because only the body is visible.

Every church or Christian organization potentially has personalities that often create chaos and confusion, who are embedded in its midst. They may appear to be cordial and well-meaning, but they may have personalities and beliefs that poses a threat to the health of a relationship, church, or organization. They often do not believe they are being difficult, and they will often believe that God is on their side and sincerely believe in their cause.

How do we manage this situation so that this potential weed of conflict and contention doesn't control and distract from the mission of the organization? How do we not respond like the ostrich when danger is in its midst? We may hope that these challenges would go away on its own. They never go away, and they will become elephants in the room that are often ignored but cannot be ignored. Churches and groups often regrettably learn to be controlled and co-exist in uncomfortable ways around this elephant. One of these types of "elephants in the room" is often referred to as *Jezebel Personalities*. The Bible speaks of this heartless woman with a contentious history that contradicted the name she was given, for Jezebel means "chaste, free from carnal connection"; but by nature, this character in scripture was a most licentious woman.

Jezebels are difficult and toxic persons who creates difficult situations because of their divisive character and personalities. They come in all shapes, sizes, cultures, sexes, and economic status. They have quiet and unassuming, or dominant personalities. They are introverts and they are extroverts. They may be aggressive or passive-aggressive personalities. We will see, later in this book, further biblical details of how this character in the Bible was a disruptive and toxic influence in her time. Let's look at some of their characteristics.

Characteristics of The Types of Jezebel Personalities in a Church or Organization

Nevertheless, I have this against you: You tolerate that woman Jezebel, who calls herself a prophet. By her teaching she misleads my servants into sexual immorality and the eating of food sacrificed to idols. I have given her time to repent of her immorality, but she is unwilling. (Revelation 2:20, 21 NIV)

Bird Dog – This is the four-legged bird dog who points to where the hunter should shoot. The two-legged bird dog loves to be the pastor's eyes, ears, and nose, sniffing out items for attention.

Gloom and Doom – These persons have a negative disposition that can be contagious. They spread gloom, erase excitement, and can bog down the ministry with their negative attitudes.

Salesman – This person is enthusiastic. This person is the first to greet visitors at the church and invite them to their home. But conversely, this person is equally excited about selling any items they may have for sale as a part of their personal business.

Money Manipulator – This person uses money to register approval or disapproval of church decisions. Sometimes this person protests silently by merely withholding offerings.

Flawed Pots

Busy Body – This person enjoys telling others how to do their jobs

Sniper – This person avoids face-to-face conflict, but picks off pastors and leadership with pot shots in private conversations. "Be sure to pray for our pastor and leadership, they have some problems, you know."

Micro Manager – This person keeps a written record of everything that someone does that isn't in the "spirit of Christ."

Legalist – This is the official Pharisee of the church who is full of absolutes, from the kind of car the pastor drives to the number of verses in a hymn that must be sung. These people know the constitution and by-laws almost verbatim; they use the documents to their benefit when needed, and resort to them when they want to exert their influence.

Protectors - These people believe it's their duty to protect every church or family tradition, whether or not the tradition is still relevant. Known for phrases like "that's not the way we've always done it"

Bible Thumpers - members who elevate their own belief system above any other; they quickly point out anyone who differs in any interpretation.

Complainers - People in churches who grumble continually, carrying the assumed responsibility to leaders; as one member once said to a leader, "God uses me to keep you from getting too high on yourself."

Crusaders - Focused on only one ministry or sacred cow, these members guard their turf with all their force; consequently, they contribute to the silos that so often mark congregations.

Anonymous - People who express their opinion, but only behind the curtain of anonymity; they share concerns, but they do so with cowardice. As my parents used to say, they throw a rock and hide their hand.

Exaggerators — People who spread rumors based on what other people may have said; they generally portray a few people (sometimes even only themselves) as "some people say." **"God told me"** members who stand on what "God told me," regardless of whether what God is reported to have said contradicts His Word; they almost dare others to differ with them.

As you read through this list, I suspect you may think of some people you know (or, if you're honest, you may see yourself among this list). If so, take time to pray for them, and even for yourself. If you don't try to resolve these challenges, you will only get more frustrated, and you are contributing to the problem by being one of the difficult people, rather than helping resolve it.

Let's look again at this Jezebel character, and let us examine what makes them a challenge.

Chapter 4:
The Challenges of a Jezebel Spirit

Never get mad at someone for being who they've always been. Be upset with yourself for not coming to terms with it sooner.

I had a little bird,
Its name was Enza.
I opened the window,
And in-flu-enza.

The effect of the 1918 influenza epidemic was so severe that the average life span in the US was depressed by 10 years. The influenza virus was a profound virus, with a mortality rate of at 2.5 percent compared to the previous influenza epidemics, which were less than 0.1 percent. The death rate for 15- to 34-year-olds of influenza and pneumonia were twenty times higher in 1918 than in previous years. People were struck with illness on the street and died rapid deaths. One incident in 1918 was of four women playing bridge together late into the night. Overnight, three of the women died from influenza.

As horrific as that epidemic was in 1918, there is also a Jezebel virus and spirit that if not detected and cured, can disrupt and affect and infect the life of a home, organization and yes, even a congregation. In discerning those persons with this viral spirit, they can and will potentially suck the life out of your relationships and ministry. A Jezebel spirit or virus will slowly compromise the mission of a group. They are often persons who are skillful and tunnel-visioned. It is important to be able to effectively use all the spiritual tools before you. Wherever this spirit exists or has a foothold, whether this is in a relationship, church, organization, or home, you will potentially have a delayed, destructive, or dysfunctional situation. Let's look at the background of this destructive personality.

When you think of Jezebel, what comes to mind?

> The name Jezebel usually evokes for us an image of a woman who is sexually alluring or trying to be; a manipulator of men.
>
> A Jezebel spirit, for our example in this book, could be a male or female, and an example of someone who is into *control, power, prestige, intimidation* and having it their way.

Let's look briefly at who she was in scripture

1. *Jezebel Was into POWER (I Kings 16:31)*

   a. She married King Ahab for power (16:31-32)
   b. The marriage was political, as the Syrians were becoming a threat (alliance)

2. *She came from a powerful and treacherous family.* Her father was Ethbaal, king of Sidon (Phoenicia), a priest of Baal who assassinated the king and took over. Unlike the Jews who had a male priesthood, the Phoenicians had priestesses, so Jezebel would have been a priestess of Baal and Baal's cohort, Astarte. Astarte was a fertility goddess worshipped through temple prostitution

But it carried religious overtones: Jezebel brought in her idols, heathen temple, and a staff of Baal-worshipping priests and priestesses. So this made the Northern Kingdom of Israel, which had already departed from the Jewish Torah, more fully pagan.

3. *She had the true prophets of God executed in 1 Kings* (18:4) Jezebel and God's Prophets. Elijah, in his confrontation with her in 1 Kings 18:4,

describes Jezebel as an enemy of God who was "killing off the Lord's prophets." In response, the prophet Elijah accused King Ahab of abandoning the Lord and challenged Jezebel's 450 prophets of Baal and 450 prophets of Asherah to a contest.

They were to meet him on the top of Mt. Carmel. Then Jezebel's prophets would slaughter a bull, but not set fire to it, as required for an animal sacrifice.

Elijah would do the same on another altar. Whichever god caused the bull to catch fire would then be proclaimed as the true god. Jezebel's prophets beseeched their gods to ignite their bull, but nothing happened. When it was Elijah's turn, he soaked his bull in water, prayed, and "then the fire of the Lord fell and burned up the sacrifice." (1 Kings 18:38).

Upon seeing this miracle, the people who were watching prostrated themselves and believed that Elijah's god was the true God. Elijah then commanded the people to kill Jezebel's prophets, which they did. When Jezebel learns of this, she declares Elijah an enemy and promises to kill him, just as he killed her prophets.

4. *She promoted heathen religion (1 Kings 18:19)*
Note that they "ate at her table"

Revelation 2:20 reads:
"Nevertheless, I have this against you: You tolerate that woman Jezebel, who calls herself a prophetess. By her teaching she misleads my servants into sexual immorality and the eating of food sacrificed to idols."

5. *Jezebel overshadowed her husband*
   a. She initiated the tragedy of Naboth's vineyard (1 Kings 21:5-15)

Jezebel and Naboth's Vineyard

Although Jezebel is one of many wives, 1 Kings and 2 Kings make it apparent that she wielded a considerable amount of power. The earliest example of her influence occurs in 1 Kings 21, when her husband wanted a vineyard belonging to Naboth the Jezreelite. Naboth refused to give his land to the king because it had been in his family for generations.

In response, Ahab became sad and upset. When Jezebel noticed her husband's mood, she inquired the reason and decided to get the vineyard for Ahab. She did so by writing letters in the king's name, commanding the elders of Naboth's city to accuse him of cursing both God and his King.

The elders obliged, and Naboth was convicted of treason, then was stoned. Upon his death, his property reverted to the king, so in the end Ahab got the vineyard he wanted.

At God's command, the prophet Elijah then appeared before Ahab and Jezebel. He said that because of their actions *"This is what the LORD says: In the place where dogs licked up Naboth's blood, dogs will lick up your blood - yes, yours!"* (1 Kings 21:17).

He further prophesies that Ahab's male descendants will die, his dynasty will end, and that dogs will *"devour Jezebel by the wall of Jezreel."* (1 Kings 21:23).

b. She incited her husband, Ahab, to great evil (1 Kings 21:25)

6. *Difficult people often face a life of consequences* (2 Kings 9:30-37)

Elijah's prophesy at the end of the vineyard story comes true when Ahab dies in Samaria and his son, Ahaziah, dies within two years of ascending the throne. He is killed by Jehu, who emerges as another contender for the throne when the prophet Elisha declares him King. Here again, Jezebel's influence becomes apparent. Though Jehu has killed the king, he has to kill Jezebel in order to assume power.

According to 2 Kings 9:30-34, Jezebel and Jehu meet soon after the death of her son Ahaziah. When she learns of his death, she puts on make-up, does her hair, and looks out a palace window, only to see Jehu enter the city.

She calls to him, and he responds by asking her servants if they are on his side. "Who is on my side?

Who?" he asks, "Throw her down!" (2 Kings 9:32). Jezebel's eunuchs then betray her by throwing her out the window. She dies when she hits the street and is trampled by horses. After taking a break to eat and drink, Jehu commands that she be buried "for she was a king's daughter" (2 Kings 9:34), but by the time his men go to bury her, dogs have eaten all but her skull, feet and hands.

In modern times the name "Jezebel" is often associated with an evil woman. According to some scholars, she has received such a negative reputation not only because she was a foreign princess who worshiped foreign gods, but because she wielded so much power as a woman.

So, let's look into six areas in scripture concerning Jezebel. How do we develop the wisdom and courage to confront difficult persons in our midst with a Jezebel spirit?

Suggested Process of Confronting a Jezebel Spirit

1.Fight a Jezebel Spirit with the power of prayer.
The most common targets of Jezebels are the leaders and church staff.

I encourage everyone in vocational ministry to ask humbly for people to pray for them daily. One staff leader stated that in two of the churches where they served as staff, they had as many as one hundred or more people committed to pray for him daily. They typically prayed for him for only two or three minutes each day at noon. Their intercessory prayers were brief, but they were powerful and gave him wisdom.

2. Seek to have an Acts 6 group in the church.

I am specifically referring to the manner in which the Jerusalem church dealt with murmuring and complaining. They appointed a group to take care of the widows who were being overlooked in the daily distribution of food. The seven who were appointed to the task were not only to do that important ministry, but they were also to preserve the unity of the church. Churches need to consider either informal or formal groups that see their ministry as dealing with conflict, complaints, and dissension, so that unity is preserved.

3. Have a high-expectation church or organization.

Higher expectation churches tend to be more unified, more Great Commission focused, more biblically defined, and more servant oriented. Stated simply, high-expectation churches don't offer an environment conducive to Jezebels.

4. Encourage members and staff to speak and stand up to church Jezebels.

Jezebels thrive in a church where the majority remains in silent fear of church bullies. Jezebels tend to back down when confronted by strong people in the church. We just need more strong people in the church.

5. Make certain the polity of the church does not become a useful instrument to Jezebels.

Many churches have ambiguous structures and lines of accountability. When there is lack of vision and clear expectations, where the polity is weak and ill-defined, this spirit of Jezebel will exist. Jezebels take advantage of the ambiguity and interpret things according to their nefarious needs.

6. Be willing to exercise ministry discipline.

Church discipline is a forgotten essential of many churches. Jezebels need to know there are consequences for their actions, and church discipline may be one of them.

7. Have a healthy and clear process to put the best-qualified persons in positions of leadership in the church.

Jezebels are often able to push around less qualified people who have found themselves in positions of leadership. There should be a spiritually and strategically designed process to choose and recruit people for key leadership positions.

If the pastoral leadership and new staff members do not have good chemistry, a church Jezebel can quickly pit one against the other. A unified church staff is a major roadblock for a Jezebel spirit.

8. Encourage a celebratory environment in the church or group.

Joyous and healthy churches deter and limit Jezebels. Weeds in a garden have difficulty existing and growing in healthy soil. I remember when I was a pastor, we would constantly find ways to celebrate weekly and monthly, whether it was new members, celebrating the completion of class with awards and the like, recognizing the success of a ministry or person in your midst, or something similar. You can complete your own list of celebrations. One of the advantages of doing this is that it creates ministry momentum that keeps churches from flatlining.

How Does One Discern a Jezebel Spirit?

I know your deeds, your love and faith, your service and perseverance, and that you are now doing more than you did at first. Nevertheless, I have this against you: You tolerate that woman Jezebel, who calls herself a prophet. By her teaching she misleads my servants into sexual immorality and the eating of food sacrificed to idols. I have given her time to repent of her immorality, but she is unwilling. (Revelation 2:19-21 NIV)

Jezebel's Character Traits

1. **The very first, and probably most outstanding quality of a person with a Jezebel Spirit, is their undeniable, ever-present need to always be right!**

Flawed Pots

They are not humble people who seek the input of others; but have an unquenchable desire to "win" over you in everything. The secular term for the spirit of Jezebel is 'malignant narcissism,' which is difficult to cure.

2. The second thing, highest on our list, is the "Chameleon" Spirit.

They possess a spirit that allows them to appear a certain way, but not actually be that way. They will adapt to their surroundings to seem like a loving, charming, and even peaceful person, all the while trying to get a hold of your soul.

3. The third aspect is their use of seduction, deception, and manipulation.

Their tendency is to control your mind, your actions, and your destiny. They want to see how far they can involve themselves in your life, how far you are willing to allow them to go. Jezebels usually come in two categories: the active, and the passive.

4. Jezebel, in their personal and private lives. are sometimes emotionally detached; even from children, especially their own. It takes great discernment to discover it.

People with the Jezebel Spirit sometimes have the tendency to treat their own children cold and distant, rarely showing tears or emotion. They like to make sure they don't get any sympathy, because they hate weakness. They don't show much love or affection – genuine hugs, smiles, and affirmations are a rare gift.

5. Jezebels will often mix religious terms and phrases to appear godly.

Their lives do not produce godliness. Following their lives and examples will subtly lead to rebellion, anger, and strife. You will many times find a Jezebel person involved in various types of teaching activities; not only in religious settings, but also places such as schools and in various types of counseling. The reason for this is their need to be an influence on people.

6. They are masters of the "blaming game," and are extremely clever at gaining sympathy for themselves by producing convincing arguments for their case.

They usually portray themselves as fair in their assessments. They will twist and turn information to better fit them, even if it involves lying and crying, anything to make you be the responsible or guilty one.

7. Jezebel struggles to truly forgive people who offend them.

They tend to keep track of all past offenses, and they use them to their advantage when they see the need for manipulation. Their love is always conditional, making you know of the things that please them, so if you do not comply, they will reject you.

8. A Jezebel spirit will never admit any fault or wrongdoing.

If you plan to confront the Jezebel with something, you can be totally clear about your problems and your list of concerns, and yet come out on the other end totally convinced that you were the only one at fault.

9. The spirit of Jezebel brings about a tremendously powerful confusion that can make you doubt everything you stand for.

After your first few confrontations, you learn to stay away from coming even remotely close to suggesting correction. You find out, that you are not strong enough to stand up against it, and you start becoming passive. This kind of passivity is what King Ahab suffered from when he looked the other way, instead of confronting the wrong his wife, Queen Jezebel, was doing:

When Jezebel heard the news, she said to Ahab, "You know the vineyard Naboth wouldn't sell you? Well, you can have it now! He's dead!" So Ahab immediately went down to the vineyard to claim it." 1. Kings 21:15-16 NLT

10. No peace around Jezebel

I believe we have to understand that dealing with the Jezebel spirit will never be peaceful! One of you will give in, and that is certainly not going to be Jezebel, if they have their way. The only way a Jezebel spirit exist and festers in a home, group, or an organization is to have a passive Ahab spirit present. There was a Hollywood actress who recently found herself frustrated being around her former girlfriend. Listen to her response to this strained relationship:

"I feel, like at this point, I am paying attention now. I see things for exactly how they are. I am not confused about my relationship or even had a relationship with this woman. She continued, "I deserve better. At this point, this is not a healthy thing for me. This is not a healthy person for me. This is not a healthy person for me to be around. This is not good for my spirit. I am all about affirmation and peace. I do not want to tear women down. I want to lift them up."

Signs That Your Ministry or Organization Has a Jezebel Spirit

Recently, I have come across people in unhealthy situations. Having worked in some of these settings, I have seen patterns that have led me to start thinking. Here lies the problem of some dysfunctional organizations, homes, and churches. It often does good things on the outside while destroying the souls of those on the inside. So, how do you know if where you live, work, or serve has a Jezebel Spirit? Let me share just a few to reveal the many signs that I have observed:

1. The culture of the group sometimes does not value those serving; just those leading.
2. The leader of the group is the only one allowed to think.
3. The organization, church, or home thinks everyone else is wrong, and only they are right.

4. People rationalize that the good they are experiencing is worth the abuse they are receiving.
5. People know the glaring difficulties of the leader, church member, friend, or family member, but no one can or will speak truth to power.
6. Many times the leader reluctantly gets a pass from others for their poor leadership because of some overwhelming characteristic; for example, their preaching or teaching ability, intelligence, ability to woo others, their position in the community, their wealth, overbearing personality, the dark secrets they have over everyone's life, etc.

Potential Toxic Leaders in Churches

1. Leaders who don't spend enough time in prayer.

2. Leaders who don't take a hard, realistic look at themselves on a regular basis.

3. Leaders who blame everyone else in the church organization except themselves.

4. Leaders who haven't figured out how to work collaboratively with other leaders.

5. Leaders who don't spend enough time in preparation and study of the scriptures.

6. Leaders who believe everyone works for them, rather than this leader becoming a servant to others.

7. Leaders who don't have mentors in their lives who hold them accountable.

8. Leaders who believe it is always other people's fault for why their church is not fruitful.

9. Leaders who don't spend enough time with their people and leaders.

10. Leaders who have unresolved issues in their personal and home life, and it leaks and creates dysfunction within their congregation.

11. Leaders who socially live in isolation and function in their personal life as loners.

12. Leaders who have too much time on their hands and don't use their time effectively.

13. Leaders who don't have an evangelistic or pastoral heart.

14. Leaders who are unable to adapt to the changing reality and culture around them.

Here is a quote from one of my favorite authors, and one of the great writers in literature, that reveals a poignant reality:

"Not everything that is faced changes; but nothing is changed unless it is faced." James Baldwin

Chapter 5:
Fighting Righteously

"If your only tool is a hammer, you will see every problem as a nail."
Gambian proverb

A man heard his daughter and some of her friends arguing loudly in the back yard. He went out and reprimanded her. "But, Daddy," she protested, "we were just playing church."

It's sad, but true, that the church of Jesus Christ has often been marked more by factions than by fellowship. There is even a book titled Great Church Fights. On page 117, it observes, "In the history of the church, we have seen that when the devil could not destroy the church by persecution, the next thing he did was to join it!" If you have been a Christian for very long, you have probably been in a church that went through a major fight or a split.

Dr. Donald Davenport

In this fallen world, some splits are inevitable if we are committed to sound doctrine and godly standards. There have always been, and always will be, those who bring in destructive beliefs (2 Pet. 2:1) and/or evil behavior (2 Pet. 2:13-14, 18-19). If church leaders choose to be obedient to God, they must confront serious errors and sinful behavior (Titus 1:9-16). But when they do so, even if they follow the Scripture and act in love, there are always some who will react negatively and leave.

No matter what the cause of the disunity, we should work at resolving conflicts in the church in a biblical manner. Paul tells us to be diligent "to preserve the unity of the Spirit in the bond of peace" (Eph. 4:3). We should "pursue the things which make for peace and the building up of one another" (Rom. 14:19). If we want God's blessing, Peter says that we "must seek peace and pursue it" (1 Pet. 3:11b). Passivity is not adequate. We must pursue peace in a godly manner, without compromising truth or holiness.

Nehemiah Pursuing Peace in the Midst of Conflict
Nehemiah 5:1-19
"Now the men and their wives raised a great outcry against their fellow Jews. Some were saying, "We and our sons and daughters are numerous; in order for us to eat and stay alive, we must get grain." Others were saying, "We are mortgaging our fields, our vineyards and our homes to get grain during the famine." Still others were saying, "We have had to borrow money to pay the king's tax on our fields and vineyards. Although we are of the same flesh and blood as our fellow Jews and though our children are as good

as theirs, yet we have to subject our sons and daughters to slavery. Some of our daughters have already been enslaved, but we are powerless, because our fields and our vineyards belong to others." When I heard their outcry and these charges, I was very angry. I pondered them in my mind and then accused the nobles and officials. I told them, "You are charging your own people interest!" So I called together a large meeting to deal with them and said: "As far as possible, we have bought back our fellow Jews who were sold to the Gentiles.

Now you are selling your own people, only for them to be sold back to us!" They kept quiet, because they could find nothing to say. So I continued, "What you are doing is not right. Shouldn't you walk in the fear of our God to avoid the reproach of our Gentile enemies? I and my brothers and my men are also lending the people money and grain. But let us stop charging interest! Give back to them immediately their fields, vineyards, olive groves and houses, and also the interest you are charging them—one percent of the money, grain, new wine and olive oil." "We will give it back," they said. "And we will not demand anything more from them. We will do as you say."

Then I summoned the priests and made the nobles and officials take an oath to do what they had promised. I also shook out the folds of my robe and said, "In this way may God shake out of their house and possessions anyone who does not keep this promise. So may such a person be shaken out and emptied!" At this the whole assembly said,

"Amen," and praised the Lord. And the people did as they had promised. Moreover, from the twentieth year of King Artaxerxes, when I was appointed to be their governor in the land of Judah, until his thirty-second year—twelve years—neither I nor my brothers ate the food allotted to the governor. But the earlier governors—those preceding me—placed a heavy burden on the people and took forty shekels of silver from them in addition to food and wine. Their assistants also lorded it over the people. But out of reverence for God I did not act like that. Instead, I devoted myself to the work on this wall. All my men were assembled there for the work; we did not acquire any land. Furthermore, a hundred and fifty Jews and officials ate at my table, as well as those who came to us from the surrounding nations. Each day one ox, six choice sheep and some poultry were prepared for me, and every ten days an abundant supply of wine of all kinds. In spite of all this, I never demanded the food allotted to the governor, because the demands were heavy on these people. Remember me with favor, my God, for all I have done for these people."

Nehemiah did not have smooth sailing in trying to rebuild the walls of Jerusalem, as chapter 3 by itself might lead us to believe. Chapters 4 and 6 show how he had to face opposition from without. Chapter 5 shows how he had to deal with conflict from within his group. Some scholars argue that these events must have taken place after the wall was completed, since Nehemiah would not have taken the time for an assembly of the whole populace (5:7) in the middle of the project. But my understanding is that he did have to take the time in the middle of the project to deal with this internal problem that threatened to sabotage the work.

The problem (5:1-5) centered on the complaints of the poorer Jews against the wealthy Jews, who were either ignoring their desperate needs or were actually making those needs worse through exploiting them. Things were made worse by a famine, so that those who owned property were forced to mortgage their fields, vineyards, and houses in order to get food. Others had to borrow in order to pay the king's tax on their lands. Some were even forced to sell their children into slavery to their fellow Jews in order to pay their bills.

They were in disregard of the Mosaic law that forbade a Jew from loaning money at interest to a fellow Jew in need (Exod. 22:25; Deut. 23:19); the wealthier Jews were not only charging interest, but they were also taking Jewish children as slaves, as collateral for the loans. They were operating as heartless businessmen, putting their own financial gain first, without regard for how it hurt their poorer brethren and their families.

Nehemiah saw these problems as serious enough to stop the work on the wall long enough to get them resolved. The way he dealt with things and the people's response show us some biblical principles for resolving conflicts in the church. In order to do God's work, we must resolve difficult conflicts in the church in a biblical manner. Let me emphasize again: in a biblical manner.

Dr. Donald Davenport

There are three principles here, two of which involve the people, and one that involves the leaders.

1. To resolve conflicts biblically, people must air complaints to the proper channels and authorities.

We do not know whether the people who were being wronged had first gone to those exploiting them without getting things resolved. That is always the first step when you think that someone has wronged you, to go *directly* to the person and try to get things resolved (Matt. 18:15). But at this point, they brought their complaint to Nehemiah, or at least he heard about it. There is a basic and yet often overlooked principle: a leader cannot deal with problems that they are not aware of. Sometimes they cannot deal with problems, even when they are aware of them, of course. But without exception, it is impossible to deal with problems when you do not know about them.

I am amazed at how often people air their complaints to everyone except the leaders, who could perhaps do something to help. They always have an excuse: "I just wanted to see if anyone else felt the same way that I feel." Or, "I just need to air my feelings." Or, "The pastor is too busy, and he won't listen to you anyway!" So they circulate through the church, stirring up dissension and disunity, but the leaders don't even know that there is a problem. As a result, the church or organization has to exist with an undercurrent spirit of hostility in their midst that becomes, over time, a dark cloud over the ministry.

Flawed Pots

Years ago, the wife of one pastor called and asked, "Did you know that Miss Jones, an elderly woman in the church, is calling through the church directory, asking people if they like us using guitars in our worship times?" He said, "No, I had no idea." So he went to visit Miss Jones. Her first words were, "So have you come to bawl me out?" He said, "No, I've come to talk with you and to explain why we have changed our music style. And I've come to ask you not to stir up gossip and controversy by calling through our church directory." Clearly, she was very uncomfortable with such direct resolution of a problem.

But to talk to everyone in the church except those who can do something about the problem just stirs up dissension and spreads gossip. To resolve conflicts or problems biblically, go directly to the person responsible and talk about the problem. If someone comes to you with a complaint, ask if they have talked to one of the pastors or leaders. If not, direct him to do so before he talks to anyone else. Many misunderstandings can be resolved at this level without causing larger problems in the church.

2. To resolve conflicts biblically, leaders must deal with complaints in a biblical manner.

Nehemiah is an example of godly leadership here. He could have told these people, "I'm busy on this wall. Come back in six weeks, and we'll talk." But Nehemiah realized that the problems were significant, and the people were upset. So he interrupted his attention on the wall to listen and help resolve this matter. He did five things that leaders should do in difficult moments with difficult people:

(1) He got righteously angry.

It may surprise some to read (5:6) that Nehemiah got very angry when he heard these complaints. There seem to be two extremes in Christian circles today. Some think that all anger is wrong. Sometimes Christians who think this deny their own anger, even when it is evident to everyone else. Others, buying into modern psychology, say that anger isn't right or wrong—it just is. They say that we should express it and own up to it.

The Bible clearly teaches that most anger is sinful, but that some anger is righteous (Eph. 4:26,31). Jesus got angry at the hardness of heart of the Pharisees (Mark 3:5), but He did not sin. If our anger is directed against the sinful treatment of others, and if we allow it to move us toward constructive means to try to resolve the problem, it may be righteous anger. If it involves some wrong committed against us, it may be righteous, but sinful selfishness and pride are probably mixed in with it, and so we should be very careful to examine our motives before God. Listen, just because we *can* do something, doesn't mean we *should*. It is right to get angry about sinful practices such as child abuse, pornography, abortion, racism, and the mistreatment of women. It would be sinful to respond with violence toward those who perpetrate such sins. We need to check ourselves to make sure that we direct our righteous anger righteously. That's what Nehemiah did.

(2) He exercised self-control.

Before Nehemiah contended with the ones guilty of exploiting the poor, he consulted with himself (5:7). That is significant! He didn't go off in a rage to blast those who were wrong. He stopped, cooled off, thought and prayed things through, and only then took action. Proverbs 16:32 says, "He who is slow to anger is better than the mighty, and he who rules his spirit, than he who captures a city." We all, but especially leaders, need to exercise self-control when we get angry.

(3) He followed the principles of biblical confrontation.

It's easy to get angry, but then to cool off and do nothing. After all, it is difficult and uncomfortable to confront those who are causing a problem. It is especially difficult to confront those who happen to be rich and powerful, as these men were. What if they got defensive and withdrew their support of the project? What if they began to view Nehemiah as an enemy? They could use their clout to cause a lot more damage. Maybe Nehemiah should stall for time until the wall was finished. But he didn't do that.

First, he privately confronted those guilty of mistreating the poor (5:7). We do not know whether this involved a single meeting or a series of meetings, and whether Nehemiah was alone or whether he took some trusted leaders with him.

But the biblical pattern for resolving conflict is, "If your brother sins, go and show him his fault in private; if he listens to you, you have won your brother. But if he does not listen to you, take one or two more with you" (Matt. 18:15-16a). While Nehemiah did not have our Lord's teaching on this, he seems to have followed this pattern of private confrontation before any public confrontation.

Did Nehemiah succeed in private? We don't know for sure, but probably not. There is no recorded response at this point. So Nehemiah moved to public confrontation.

He called a great assembly and spelled out the problem. He rebuked the leaders (5:8) by pointing out how he and others had redeemed their Jewish brothers who had been sold to the nations, but now it was Jews themselves who were selling their brothers into slavery. They could not find a word to answer. He further stated that their behavior was not good in that their enemies would mock the Jews for their mistreatment of their own people (5:9).

Some think that Nehemiah (5:10) is admitting his own past failure in lending money at interest to his fellow Jews (based on the plural "let us leave off the usury"), but I think that he is just using the plural to identify with these men. Nehemiah had loaned money in accordance with the Law, without charging interest. He is appealing to these wealthy men to join him in doing the same. He asks them to give back to the poor their fields, vineyards, olive groves, and houses, along with the interest that they had charged.

There are many Christians and leaders who are afraid to confront people with bad behaviors with their sin, whether in private or in public. This fear increases when the person with toxic behavior is rich and powerful. But we must follow Nehemiah's example of confronting those who are in sin. Nehemiah exhibited proper righteous anger under control. His anger gave him the courage to confront those who were wrong.

(4) He set a personal example of godliness.

One reason that Christians hesitate to confront those in sin is the fear that the one confronted will point his finger back at the one doing the confronting, exposing areas where he is in sin. So they say, "Judge not, lest you be judged," and let things go.

Nehemiah shows us that leaders must be above reproach, proving to be examples to the flock (1 Pet. 5:1-4). He had spent his own money to redeem fellow Jews from slavery (5:8). He had loaned them money without interest (5:10). We don't know at what point Nehemiah had been appointed governor, whether before he went to Jerusalem the first time, or sometime after the wall was finished. But in 5:14-19, he adds his own example as governor over a twelve-year period, not out of pride, but to give an example for other leaders to follow. His practices give us several important principles for leaders.

(a) He laid aside his rights and did not take advantage of his position and power (5:14-15).

He rightly could have demanded a food allowance, as his predecessors had done, by taxing the people and then sending their servants out to collect the tax with force. The governor had a right to such an allowance, and Nehemiah could have imposed it. After all, he had a hundred and fifty Jews and officials at his table daily, besides those who came in from surrounding nations (5:17). To feed them required one ox and six choice sheep, plus poultry and wine every day (5:18). But Nehemiah set aside his right to the governor's food allowance and apparently sacrificed these costs out of his own pocket.

Many Christians and leaders fall into the trap of thinking that their position gives them certain rights and power. We should follow the example of the Lord Jesus, who laid aside His rights to take on the form of a servant and be obedient, even to death on a cross.

(b) He feared God and cared about hurting people (5:15b, 18b).

Nehemiah gives two reasons why he resisted the trend of his predecessors and laid aside his rights: He feared God (5:15b), and he was concerned "because the servitude was heavy on this people" (5:18b). Every person in leadership must constantly remember that they are only a servant under God, and that they must answer to God someday. This is not "my" church; it is Christ's church, and I am just His under-shepherd. Fearing God means that we should not do things as others, even other Christians, do them. We must fear God

Flawed Pots

first and foremost. And we must care about hurting people. To add to the burden of those who are already burdened would be insensitive and unloving.

Years ago, there was a man who had a beautiful 1968 Mustang. His office was at home. One day, he listened to a woman who had all sorts of problems. He offered some counsel and prayed with her. As she left, he was standing at the window and watched as she backed her huge car into his nice Mustang. He saw the Mustang move when she hit it and he winced, but apparently she didn't even feel it, because she drove off. He could have called her and asked that she submit the incident to her insurance, but he thought, "She's got enough problems already." He thought, "Lord, she just hit my car!" But the Lord said, "That's okay. People matter more than cars do." So he dropped it there and lived with the dent.

(c) He was generous and ready to share (5:17-18).

It cost him to feed everyone out of his own pocket, but he was willing to do it so that he didn't have to impose a burden on these already burdened people. He understood that he needed to be an example of generosity.

(d) He was committed to the work (5:16).

Nehemiah reports that he applied himself (or "held fast") to the work on the wall, and neither he nor his servants bought any land. Nehemiah and his servants probably knew in advance that real estate prices would shoot up once the wall was completed.

They could have bought up land cheaply before announcing the project, and then sold the land at a tidy profit. But the soldier in active service does not get entangled in everyday affairs, so that he may please the one who enlisted him (2 Tim. 2:4). Nehemiah kept his focus on the work. So should we.

(e) He worked for God's approval (5:19).

Nehemiah was not working for man's applause, but for God's "well done." "He mentions it to God in prayer not as if he thought he had merited any favor from God, as a debt, but to show that he did not look for any payback of his generosity from men, but depended upon God only to make up to him what he had lost and laid out for his honor; and he reckoned the favor of God enough." We all should seek God's approval, even if people do not say "thanks."

So, Nehemiah exercised righteous anger under control. He confronted those at fault biblically. He set a godly personal example. The remarkable thing is that when he confronted them with their wrong behavior, they agreed to give back the money and do as Nehemiah had requested (5:12). But Nehemiah didn't say, "That's wonderful, God bless you!" He did something else that leaders must do:

(5) He required accountability

Nehemiah knew that human nature is full of good intentions that never make it into practice. So he made these rich men take a public oath before the priests that they would follow through. Then, in the tradition of the prophets, he dramatically shook out his robe in front of them and said, "Thus may God shake out every man from his house and from his possessions who does not fulfill this promise; even thus may he be shaken out and emptied" (5:13). He was holding them accountable.

The organization need to hold people accountable to their promises before God and others. If there has been marital unfaithfulness or financial misdeeds, the guilty party needs to reestablish trust. The only way to do that is through very close accountability.

To resolve conflicts biblically, people must air complaints to the proper authorities. Leaders must deal with those complaints in a biblical manner. Finally:

3. To resolve conflicts biblically, people must be willing to submit to God, to His Word, and to godly leaders.

Sadly, when leaders confront people with wrongdoing, all too often the people either react with anger and defensiveness, or they just move on to another church or drop out of church altogether, without dealing with their sinful behavior.

But thankfully, there are a few victories, such as we see here. These rulers accepted Nehemiah's rebuke without fighting back. They could see that their behavior disobeyed God's Word, it hurt their fellow Jews, and it gave their enemies cause to mock them and their God (5:9). They were willing to face up to their own greed, and to pay back those whom they had taken advantage of. And they were not only willing to be held accountable, but they did it with praise to God (5:13). It's a wonder that Nehemiah didn't fall over with a heart attack!

Dealing with Mean and Difficult People with Empathy and Humility

Empathy
The first proper response to difficult people is empathy, especially when it is a first-time altercation or offense. This is a gentle attempt to understand and relate to the pain behind the meanness, and is much more effective than combativeness in dispelling a conflict. One of the most beautiful examples of empathy in the Bible is Jesus' response to those who crucified Him and cast lots for His clothing. This is a dramatic example, because what was being done to Jesus was way beyond meanness—it was torture and injustice. Instead of focusing on His own pain, He thought of their spiritual condition. Instead of responding with justified anger, He asked God to forgive them for their ignorant actions (Luke 23:34). Stephen, the church's first martyr, followed that example (Acts 7:59–60).

Humility
A little humility often goes a long way. Maybe even to the point of preserving your household or organization. Often in the spirit of humility, the question may mean asking what is ultimately in the best interests of not just me and my needs, but rather the bigger picture of my home, church, or organization.

The sober truth is that sometimes, you are the difficult person. The challenge is to not be like the unforgiving servant in Jesus' parable in Matthew 18:21–35. A servant owed a huge debt to his master; it was an amount he could never pay back. The story goes to say that the master completely wiped out the debt. The servant, however, went to another servant who owed him a small amount of money and demanded that he pay up—and when the debtor could not pay, he threw him in prison! The master heard about it and became angry. The master reinstated the unforgiving servant's original debt and threw him in jail. Humility reminds us that we should always try to remember, when people are mean to us, that we owe God a huge debt. He forgave us, and we can forgive others.

Difficult Personality of a Spouse

The Bible also tells us of a married couple named Abigail and Nabal. Unfortunately, she married a man who had a very difficult personality. The scriptures describe him as being a hard man who did evil things. I imagine he was difficult in his tone and harsh attitude toward her on a daily basis. It is not easy living with someone who regularly complains and intimidates us daily with their harsh attitude. The bible describes Abigail as intelligent and attractive. Here is how the Bible in 1 Samuel 25 describes them:

There was a man in Maon who did business in Carmel. He was a very important man and owned three thousand sheep and one thousand goats.... The man's name was Nabal, and his wife's name was Abigail. She was an intelligent and attractive woman, but her husband was a hard man who did evil things... 1 Samuel 25:2-3 (CEB)

Because of his difficult personality, he was very offensive in his words to King David, who came to his house and merely wanted some food to eat for him and his men because of their long day of travel, and they were very hungry.

"David's men delivered this message to Nabal in David's name. Then they waited there, and Nabal finally answered, "David? Who is he? I've never heard of him! The country is full of runaway slaves nowadays! I'm not going to take my bread and water, and the animals I have slaughtered for my shearers, and give them to people who come from I don't know where!"
1 Samuel 25:9-11 GNB

David expected a little more hospitality from the head of this household. David became enraged and was on the verge of destroying him and his entire household. It was his wife Abigail's actions of humility that protected the home, in spite of her husband.

When Abigail heard what her husband had done, she flew into action! She began baking cakes and bread, gathering sheep and wine. She prepared a feast and loaded it all on donkeys. She set out to meet David and his men. But she didn't tell Nabal what she was doing.

Finally, Abigail meets up with David. She jumps off her donkey and falls at his feet.

Flawed Pots

"Put the blame on me, my master! ... Here is a gift, which your servant has brought to my master. ...Please forgive any offense by your servant. When the LORD has done good things for my master, please remember your servant." 1 Samuel 25:24-31 (CEB)

Abigail is willing to take the blame for her husband's sins, for his evil, for his failure to meet the basic needs of another person. He had placed his entire household in danger. She was willing to take the blame for actions that she was completely unaware of at first, actions that would have had harsh consequences for her and her entire household.

David said to Abigail, "Bless the LORD God of Israel, who sent you to meet me today! And bless you and your good judgment for preventing me from shedding blood and taking vengeance into my own hands today! ... Then David accepted everything she had brought for him. "Return home in peace," he told her. "Be assured that I've heard your request and have agreed to it."
1 Samuel 25:32-35 (CEB)

When Abigail humbly and successfully prevented David from slaughtering Nabal, she went to tell her husband and found him so drunk that she had to wait until morning to talk to him. Alcohol was his drug of choice, and he became totally debilitated because he couldn't kick his habit.

When Abigail finally told Nabal how she had successfully intervened in his life, and how David was angry to the point of destroying his household, Nabal's heart "died within him so that he became as a stone" (v. 37). His physical condition mirrored his spiritual deadness. His stubborn refusal to submit to God's authority ended up taking him to an early grave.

Chapter 6:
These People Can Be Frustrating

Sometimes the very people that rub us the wrong way may be the aggravating heavenly sandpaper God is using to smooth out the rough edges in our own hearts.

Passive-aggressiveness is a learned response from a home life dynamic, experienced and learned in youth. Passive-aggressiveness includes the obvious passive, withdrawn, or apathetic approach to relationships. These personalities can become difficult and frustrating, because they don't always reveal, or be honest with themselves or to others what they are really believing and feeling.

8 Examples of passive aggressive behavior
- *Resenting the demands of others. ...*
- *Deliberate procrastination. ...*
- *Intentional mistakes. ...*
- *Hostile attitude. ...*
- *Complaints of injustice and lack of appreciation. ...*

- *Disguising criticism with compliments. ...*
- *The last punch. ...*
- *The silent treatment.*

The adult passive-aggressive often grew up in a home with too many rules to count; strict, regimented laws with no chance at personal adventures. Youth who grow up like this come to believe that speaking their truth, or simply saying 'no' to something they don't want to do, is dangerous and will jeopardize their chance to receive love and affection from their parents or caregivers.

This cycle will continue into adulthood, if never addressed. This passive-aggressive approach will spill over into all sort of adult relationships, from friendships, intimate partners, and school on to the workplace. Passive-aggressiveness never serves anyone well and will only harm the passive-aggressive persons themselves, along with those relationships they truly wish to cultivate.

Consequences of a Passive-Aggressive Spirit That Was Not Confronted

Absalom Spirit

We spoke earlier of a Jezebel spirit that is controlling, intimidating, and dominating. We will now see an Absalom spirit, which is a passive-aggressive spirit that manifests itself through rebellious behavior, whose goal was to take over the kingdom from his father, David. This Absalom spirit was initiated out of being wounded, hurt, and bitter from prior unresolved family matters from David the father, and not David the king.

Setting themselves up through influencing people
1 Samuel 15: 1-12

"In the course of time, Absalom provided himself with a chariot and horses and with fifty men to run ahead of him. He would get up early and stand by the side of the road leading to the city gate. Whenever anyone came with a complaint to be placed before the king for a decision, Absalom would call out to him, "What town are you from?" He would answer, "Your servant is from one of the tribes of Israel." Then Absalom would say to him, "Look, your claims are valid and proper, but there is no representative of the king to hear you." And Absalom would add, "If only I were appointed judge in the land! Then everyone who has a complaint or case could come to me and I would see that they receive justice." Also, whenever anyone approached him to bow down before him, Absalom would reach out his hand, take hold of him and kiss him. Absalom behaved in this way toward all the Israelites who came to the king asking for justice, and so he stole the hearts of the people of Israel.

Deceptive in his relationship with the king, who was his father
At the end of four years, Absalom said to the king, "Let me go to Hebron and fulfill a vow I made to the Lord. While your servant was living at Geshur in Aram, I made this vow: "If the Lord takes me back to Jerusalem, I will worship the Lord in Hebron." The king said to him, "Go in peace."

Conspiracy of gathering alliances
So he went to Hebron. Then Absalom sent secret messengers throughout the tribes of Israel to say, "As soon as you hear the sound of the trumpets, then say, 'Absalom is king in Hebron.' Two hundred men from Jerusalem had accompanied Absalom. They had been invited as guests and went quite innocently, knowing nothing about the matter."

Acting religious and influencing key people
While Absalom was offering sacrifices, he also sent for Ahithophel the Gilonite, David's counselor, to come from Giloh, his hometown. And so the conspiracy gained strength, and Absalom's following kept on increasing."

We see later in scripture, as a result in verse 13, David, because of his weak leadership, escaping and fleeing from his own son Absalom and abandoning his leadership.

12 ways your passive aggressiveness is slowly killing your relationships.

1. You are not letting people know how you really feel, or what you really want.

When you hold back from speaking up or clarifying where you stand on an issue, your passive-aggressiveness is triggered because you feel scared, unsafe, or concerned that doing so will mean you will no longer receive the approval of the person you want to impress or be liked by.

This passive-aggressive pattern is dangerous in a relationship, because if the person you are in a relationship with doesn't know what you really think or want, they are not really in a relationship with you, as you truly are. With time, this only becomes more detrimental to your relationship.

You will feel resentment at living as a phony and forcing yourself to walk on eggshells, and they will feel they don't really know you. And in fact, they don't. These are two very big relationship red flags, and some of the worst feelings one can feel in any relationship: unaddressed resentment and communicating like a stranger.

2. You are forfeiting special connections with people you like out of fear of conflict

Passive-aggressiveness always chooses conflict avoidance, because you have come to experience conflict or disagreement as terrifying. It doesn't have to be. Your past may have provided limited occasions for self-expression.

The passive-aggressive certainly wants to connect with those they admire and respect, but often feel they have no tools to do so. When you, as a passive-aggressive, begin to feel attachment or real love for one who has inspired you, it's common practice to retreat and forfeit the connection because of fear that something will go wrong, or through perceived rejection. Passive-aggressive people will often break their own hearts, constantly giving up on relationships or experiences that open them up to any potential for failure, intimacy, or heightened risk of rejection, even though it's the very relationship or experience they truly want to pursue.

The American Psychiatric Association's Diagnostic and Statistical Manual of Mental Disorders (DSM) has classified passive-aggressiveness as many things throughout the years. It first appeared in 1952. Since then, it's been called a "personality style", "hidden hostility", a "defense mechanism", a "personality disorder", and "negativistic." Regardless of how you view it, or which title you prefer, it's a confusing and harmful defense that leaves both sides less clear on their relationship. This cloudy communication style is detrimental to any relationship.

3. You are giving up before you try

Many people hear their parents' opinions in their head before they made a decision. They will step away from their own dreams, desires, or other exciting prospects because they could hear their parents' critiques instead of their own. One person I know was filled with fear whenever they had to make a firm plan or answer to a pressing matter. Accepting advice from family is not an inherently bad thing. Of course, hearing out others' counsel can be very beneficial. But when others' opinions on what is "right", "good", or "appropriate", or what they would do in their own life, consistently surpasses your own, you are not developing your own soul compass and decision-making skills.

You are living an inauthentic existence. You are experiencing life through others, and not even attempting things you want to do because your parents, other family members, friends, or colleagues told you that you will fail.

4. You keep choosing the "easy" way out because you think it will avoid pain.

If you identify as passive-aggressive or are starting to think you may be, or are experiencing, passive-aggressiveness in your relationships or decision-making, you are familiar with doing things sub-par, half-hearted, or out of convenience, the choice that you believe provides you with minimal discomfort or pain. You think it's "easy," but it's not. You believe that this way you won't expose yourself too much. The fear always lurking around the corner for a passive-aggressive is that succeeding or going out on a limb will open them up to rejection, failure, ridicule, or criticism. Passive-aggressiveness will always stunt your spirit.

5. You are mistaking an honest and respectful dialogue with malicious confrontation.

Any direct dialogue, to some degree, is a terrifying prospect to a passive-aggressive person. All dialogue is confused with pain, discomfort, and other overwhelming emotions of the past. Confrontation, in almost any form, is a trigger for the passive-aggressive. It can make them recall their childhood or other experiences of their past, when confrontation was peppered with insults and obscenities or an unresponsive party. What the passive-aggressive doesn't quite understand is that being assertive, not aggressive, can help empower a bond or relationship. If the passive-aggressive goes out of their comfort zone and attempts to have an honest and respectful dialogue, and is met with resistance or abusive tactics, there may be other issues at play in the relationship that are being ignored. It's not uncommon for the passive-aggressive to get involved with co-dependents, narcissists, domineering and demanding or other inappropriate partners due to their passivity and low self-esteem.

6. You are imagining the worst-case scenario, even when things are positive in a relationship.

Passive-aggressive persons are often seen by those who know them as complainers who never make any changes. They can be contrary, fatalistic, and overall negative. According to The Angry Smile workbook, a passive-aggressive individual may make comments like "It doesn't pay to be good" or "Good things don't last." Passive-aggressive people have come to believe that not only does the worst-case scenario always happen to them, but that it's what they deserve. This is another example of the damaged self-confidence of a passive-aggressive. This makes me think of the words of Mark Twain: "I am an old man and have known a great many troubles, but most of them never happened."

7. You keep recycling old ways of dealing with complicated situations.

Because the passive-aggressive doesn't think they have many tools to deal with the ups and downs of relationships, they rely on old patterns, or what they saw parents or siblings or friends do in their relationships. If you let it, the cycle will continue on with no end. Don't recycle the same lines you used in a past relationship. Not only is it dishonest, but it prevents you from being present and aware of the relationship troubles you are experiencing.

8. You prolong an annoyance or disagreement.

Passive-aggressive people are often waving like a flag in the wind. Back and forth, they sway from one direction to the other, intensely conflicted. Prolonging a decision, a change that needs to be made, or a disagreement they've ignored only morphs into a terrible beast to be slain later. The passive-aggressive sometimes hopes the problem will go away, without them having to maturely confront the issue at the hand. Your prolonging what ails you will not benefit you. You will be faced with it again days, weeks, months, or years later.

9. You are repressing, denying, and ignoring your true thoughts and feelings.

Repressing your true thoughts and feelings is dangerous. The passive-aggressive doesn't realize the harm they are inflicting upon themselves and those around them. This is another emotionally dishonest way the passive-aggressive maintains relationships. Absalom had to have had these feelings toward his father, David.

10. You are burning bridges.

Passive-aggressiveness burns bridges. It doesn't build them. They fear the end result and incorrectly believe that all ends badly "anyway, so who cares?" This is very harmful to all relationships, because it only isolates the passive person. And others feel naturally less connected to them. Passive-aggressives believe that appearing to be polite and cooperative on the surface is the same as building good rapport with others. All the while, their true opinions are festering beneath the surface. This is not the same as a good relationship with others.

11. You are saying "yes" to every request, and then blaming others for making you do things you don't want to do.

In the book *The Angry Smile*, the authors write that passive - aggressive types will say yes to things they don't want to do, and then blame and resent the person for making them do something. This, like all the other behavioral patterns of a passive-aggressive, allows problems to escalate. Stop agreeing to things that you don't want to do or don't believe in, or that no longer serves you. The more yeses you utter, the deeper you fall into your passive-aggression, and the more trapped, obligated and unhappy you become.

12. You are ambivalent and indecisive, following the lead of everyone else but yourself.

Passive-aggressive persons will often look to their supervisor, parent, or spouse to tell them what to do, even though they resent it. When their supervisor, parent, or spouse changes their opinion, they are confused. What the passive-aggressive hasn't yet taken to heart is that others' ideas may change. If you rely on others to make your decisions or tell you what to do, you will never find peace. Many times, the passive-aggressive doesn't find refuge in their own heart and mind, but instead spends a great deal of energy avoiding things. Placing their direction on another person makes it hard for the passive-aggressive to find resolution.

How do we intentionally begin the process of dealing with these types of passive-aggressive personalities and other difficult people we have been discussing?

Let's see in the following chapters how we can, with a strong mind, gentle heart and discerning spirit, pursue peace and reconciliation in ways that glorify God.

Chapter 7:
How Do We Deal with Them

We all are a little broken. The last time I checked, broken crayons still color the same

1. Speak with Respect

Disagreements and misunderstandings will happen in life, but this is not an excuse to disrespect each other. The Bible tells us that we should speak to others with love, even if we have to deal strongly with them. Love and respect should be our guide. Our speech should be kind but firm when necessary.

Ephesians 4:15 *"But speaking the truth in love, may grow up into him in all things, which is the head, even Christ:"*

Proverbs 15:1 *"A soft answer turns away wrath: but grievous words stir up anger."*

Colossians 4:6 *"Let your speech be always with grace, seasoned with salt, that ye may know how ye ought to answer every man."*

a. A Biblical Pathway to Deal With Difficult People

Again, the best way to sum this all up is to deal with difficult people with love. Love the unsaved and the saved in such a way that they will want to know more about your God.

Follow the Pattern in Matthew 18

There is a distinct pattern given in Matthew 18 for confronting a problem. I believe this is primarily talking about dealing with problems among believers, but it can also be applied in many situations with unbelievers. First, you go privately to the one with whom the problem is. Secondly, you take a few people with you so that you can establish the facts, and so that it is no longer a "he said, she said" argument. Finally, if you cannot resolve the issue, then bring it to the attention of the authorities or people that you both respect and honor. Again, these verses are talking about the authority of the church, but it could also be applied to your office, home, or church situation.

Matthew 18:15-17 *"Moreover if thy brother shall trespass against thee, go and tell him his fault between thee and him alone: if he shall hear thee, thou hast gained thy brother. But if he will not hear thee, then take with thee one or two more, that in the mouth of two or three witnesses every word may be established. And if he shall neglect to hear them, tell it unto the church: but if he neglect to hear the church, let him be unto thee as an heathen man and a publican."*

b. Notice the power and process of agreement in confrontation

A biblical four-step process.

1. Go as a brother or sister in Christ and gently point out their fault. Be in prayer in not just what to say, but in how to confront this contrarian spirit. As an additional note, the timing is also important. Ask God to create the right moment for a holy confrontation. Some people describe this as a "Come to Jesus Moment."

2. If the first approach doesn't resolve the matter, set up another time and bring one or two other believers along. Determine clearly what is the end game or what you want to accomplish in this confrontation.

3. Again, if there is still resistance, go to the church leadership, elders, superintendent, or director. Be firm, and be prepared for a prolonged debate.

4. Lastly, the Bible tells us to treat them as you would a pagan or tax collector. Be prepared to resolve this by distancing yourself from this person, or this person being removed from a ministry or church.

Along the lines of this, remember that there is safety in a multitude of counselors or a small, core

Flawed Pots

group of wise friends. Find people to talk with about the problem. These should be trusted people, and not the church gossip. When talking to others about the problem, they may point out to you your own faults in the conflict. Check out Proverbs 11:14; 24:6.

2. Sometimes You Need to Walk Away

a. Sometimes it is better to walk away from an argument than to continue to dwell on it. However, this is not liberty to walk away from everything. There are things worth fighting for. But then, there are things that just **aren't worth your time**, and you should not allow these things to spoil your own relationship with the Lord.

b. You have to allow the Lord to **give you direction** on how to deal with different problems. After David was anointed king, but before he took the throne, he had to deal with Saul. God had already rejected Saul from being king over Israel. David, over time, realized that this was a fight between Saul and God.

c. David **allowed God to fight on his behalf**. This is the same man who years before stood up for God and fought on behalf of God when facing Goliath. David had wisdom on knowing when it was time to fight, and when it was time to walk away and allow God to handle the problem. We see David's point of view in the passage below:

1Samuel 24:10 NIV. *"This day you have seen with your own eyes how the Lord delivered you into my hands in the cave. Some urged me to kill you, but*

I spared you. I said, I will not lay my hands on my lord, because he is the Lord's anointed."

3. Their Argument May Not Be with You

a. Sometimes a person will take out their frustration and anger on you, when you aren't really the problem. It doesn't make you feel any better, but it may keep you from carrying a burden that isn't really yours to carry. You may represent something (Christianity, God, prior relationships, authority) that they don't like. **Try not to take the argument and conflict personally**.

b. The people said to Samuel that he was too old to be their leader. They wanted a king who could go out to war and fight with them. Samuel felt pretty bad about the situation. He went to God, depressed and complaining. God replied that the people were not angry with Samuel, but they were angry with God. They were just taking out their frustrations on the prophet.

c. The people's issue was with God, not Samuel
1 Samuel 8:7 *"And the LORD said unto Samuel, Hearken unto the voice of the people in all that they say unto thee: for they have not rejected thee, but they have rejected me, that I should not reign over them."*

4. Examine Yourself

Before we can effectively deal with the problems in others, we must first take care of ourselves. Matthew 7 gives an illustration that may seem silly, but it talks about human nature. The idea is that someone with a large piece of wood sticking out of their eye is criticizing another person who has a speck of dust in theirs. The one with the large piece of wood tries to ignore their own problem while dealing with the problems of others. Don't be that person. Present yourself to God, reflect, pray, and deal with your own faults before you try to correct others. When you humble yourself before God in confession, then you will be more gently able to handle the situation that you are in with the other person you felt offended by.

A question I often raise in my counseling sessions is - what would your biggest enemy say about you that has some measure of truth or merit?

Matthew 7:3-5 *"And why look at the splinter that is in your brother's eye, but considers not the beam that is in your own eye? Or how will you say to your brother, Let me pull out the splinter out of your eye; and, behold, a beam is in your own eye? Thou hypocrite, first cast out the beam out of your own eye; and then shall thou see clearly to cast out the splinter out of your brother's eye."*

5. Remember You Are Accountable to God

a. You are accountable to God for your own actions. You cannot control what the other person does, but you can control how you respond.

b. They too will be accountable for their actions, but not to you. They are accountable to God. God will hold you responsible for the way you act toward them. Paul admonishes us in Romans to realize that we are individually responsible for our actions, and to not intentionally cause others to stumble and fall before the Lord.

Proverbs 28:13 KJV *"He that covers his sins shall not prosper: but whoso confesses and forsakes them shall have mercy."*

Romans 14:10-13 KJV *"But why dost thou judge thy brother? or why dost thou set at nought thy brother? for we shall all stand before the judgment seat of Christ. For it is written, As I live, saith the Lord, every knee shall bow to me, and every tongue shall confess to God. So then every one of us shall give account of himself to God. Let us not therefore judge one another any more: but judge this rather, that no man put a stumbling block or an occasion to fall in his brother's way."*

6. Pray For Them

The book of 1 Corinthians is a book of conflict. Paul was having to deal with problems in the church. But he starts the book by saying he is praying for them. He certainly gave them the correction they needed, but he began with prayer. He then closes the book by asking for God's grace on the Corinthian believers.

1 Corinthians 1:3, 4 KJV *"Grace be unto you, and peace, from God our Father, and from the Lord Jesus Christ. I thank my God always on your behalf, for the grace of God which is given you by Jesus Christ;"*

Flawed Pots

1 Corinthians 16:23,24 KJV *"The grace of our Lord Jesus Christ be with you. My love be with you all in Christ Jesus. Amen."*

Matthew 5:44,45 KJV *"But I say unto you, Love your enemies, bless them that curse you, do good to them that hate you, and pray for them which despitefully use you, and persecute you; That ye may be the children of your Father which is in heaven: for he makes his sun to rise on the evil and on the good, and sends rain on the just and on the unjust."*

7. Sometimes You Must Agree To Disagree

Ignoring a problem does not make it go away. One of the greatest missionary evangelists of all time, the Apostle Paul, had a disagreement with his mentor, Barnabas. These two great men could not avoid a conflict. It is unlikely that we can too. However, they were able to deal with their conflict by agreeing to disagree on the issue. The Bible does not say who was right or wrong in the argument; it just says that they split up.

8. Sometimes two good people disagree, and God can bless the work of both differently

As a side note, Paul later wrote that he wanted a young man named John Mark (the cause of the conflict) to join him in the work, because Paul could see he was profitable.

Acts 15:37-40 NIV *"And Barnabas determined to take with them John, whose surname was Mark.*

But Paul thought not good to take him with them, who departed from them from Pamphylia, and went not with them to the work. And the contention was so sharp between them, that they departed asunder one from the other: and so Barnabas took Mark, and sailed unto Cyprus: And Paul chose Silas, and departed, being recommended by the brethren unto the grace of God."

God was able to confirm and bless each, in spite of their differences. When our hearts are right and we are not being difficult in our differences, God has a way of extending His divine hand of grace, so that His work is done.

Our Responsibility as Believers

Our new relationship to each other as believers in God's kingdom is to build and create accessibility and accountability toward one another. Most organizations, and in particular churches, do not have any clear and understood pathways of dealing with difficult and toxic believers, and so as a result, the elephant in the room continues to sit, poison, and infect the rest of the "Body of Christ" gradually over time.

A. Galatians 6:1-2 NIV This reveals what **we** should do.

"Brothers and sisters, if someone is caught in a sin, you who live by the Spirit should restore that person gently. But watch yourselves, or you also may be tempted. Carry each other's burdens, and in this way you will fulfill the law of Christ."

B.Isaiah 22:17-19 NIV This reveals what **God** will do

"Beware, the LORD is about to take firm hold of you and hurl you away, you mighty man. He will roll you up tightly like a ball and throw you into a large country. There you will die and there the chariots you were so proud of will become a disgrace to your master's house. I will depose you from your office, and you will be ousted from your position."

It is wonderful to know that God is on the side of the righteous, and that God will become the enemy of your enemies.

Chapter 8:
Steps to Loving Unlovable People

We have two choices when we have been hurt. We can either rehearse it or release it.

As Christians, how do we cope with difficult people? Christ calls us to love selflessly and ceaselessly. So are we just supposed to force a smile and fake a laugh, while inside we're cringing or crying or wanting to run away? How can we possibly be genuine with all these negative emotions broiling just beneath the surface?

1. Pray for the Holy Spirit's intervention.
If you know you're about to enter into an interaction with a difficult person, appeal through prayer to the Holy Spirit for strength, compassion, and patience.

2. Consult God's Word. Scripture is a treasure of practical advice about how to interact with people.

3. You don't know their whole story.
Knowing the hardships in someone's life can give you an entirely new perspective and understanding of their personality.

4. It's always possible to establish common ground.
It's amazing how finding something in common with a person you take issue with can begin to bridge the chasm between you.

5. Silence is golden, so think before you speak.
Sometimes our words stumble out of our mouths before we have a chance to censor or filter them.

6. Don't take yourself too seriously. An important life skill is learning how to laugh at yourself.

7. Be open to criticism—there could be some truth in it.

8. Don't conspire against them with others.
There's nothing more tempting than blowing off steam with a group of understanding friends after an encounter with an obnoxious coworker or acquaintance.

9. Pray for discernment about whether to confront an issue or let it go.
It's difficult to know when we should call out an offense or drop it.

10. Don't go looking for trouble.

There can be something oddly satisfying about keeping an account of our enemies' sins.

11. Remember, they are God's precious creation.
Just as you have been created in God's image, so has your intrusive neighbor, your nemesis, or your over-bearing boss.

12. Love because you are loved.
Forgive because you have been forgiven. Ephesians 4:32 puts it best: *"Be kind to one another, tenderhearted, forgiving one another, just as God through Christ has forgiven you."*

Understanding People Through Their Personality
The DISC Method

DISC is a behavior assessment tool based on the DISC theory of psychologist William Moulton Marston, which centers on four different personality traits that each person has within their personality. These are Dominance (D), Influence (I), Steadiness (S), and Conscientiousness (C). This theory was then developed into a behavioral assessment. However, there are many different behavioral tools out there that assess personalities.

For me, this method gives us a simple and clear way of understanding the basically four types of people in this world and why people do what they do, and how we can approach them effectively in ways that maximizes the relationship for fuller understanding.

Flawed Pots

These four are *Dominance, Influencing, Steadiness,* and *Conscientiousness* or *Compliance.*

For further study and understanding of this assessment tool, read the many books concerning this subject. For now, here is a brief and general simple overview of how each of these persons need to be approached and confronted with their challenging behaviors, based on their unique DISC personalities.

Let's briefly look at ways of connecting with each other on a deeper level through **communication** and working through **conflicts** by understanding their DISCs. In fact, you may see something that reminds you of yourself in one of the DISCs in the descriptions given.

Being Clear in Our Communication 2 Timothy 2:15
"Present yourself approved a workman not ashamed, rightly handling the word of truth."

How do we present and handle God's truth, the truth of your present situation, and the truth about who the other person we are dealing with, in such a way that makes us approved before God? DISC gives us one way of many to approach this.

D (DOMINANCE) Be honest and clear. To get their attention, be direct and to the point. They appreciate the word of God challenging them to live a Godly life. Sell them the idea of the rewards and consequences of what they will do in the ministry. This type of person thrives on a challenge.

Apostle Paul was a high D. Acts 9 3-6

I (INFLUENCING) Be excited. This person needs someone—for example, a leader—to give clear directions in their presentation. These persons desire a word that is positive and inspirational. To capture their attention, show them alternatives to the truths and principles that you will be sharing. This person thrives on opportunities that are placed before them.

Peter was a High I. Matthew 26:31-35,69-75

S (STEADINESS) This person thrives on encouragement before confrontation is presented. This person loves to hear about the process more than the product itself. They like to hear about relationships and harmony.

Abraham was a High S. Genesis 16:1-6

C (COMPLIANCE) Be specific and accurate in your confrontation. To capture their attention, your conversation needs to be factual. It is important that you prepare your concerns in a way that shows others that you have done your homework.

Moses was a High C. Exodus 19; Exodus 3:1-22

Flawed Pots

Working Through Our Conflicts 1 Thessalonians 5:14

"*We urge you to warn those who are idle, encourage, help the weak, be patient with everyone.*"

D: This person wants you to be straight and to the point. They want to know what is on your mind. Focus on actions and how to achieve the goal. Caring confrontation may be necessary to get their attention.

Solomon was a high D. Solomon 9:1-9

I: This person is an affiliator, negotiator, persuader, and encourager. This person responds to clear instructions. Sometimes this person has a tendency to shift blame. Confrontation in the form of questions is preferable; this allows them to explain their actions.

Aaron and David were high Is. Exodus 32:21-24

S: This person responds peacefully in conflict when they sense that they are understood and accepted for who they are. When they sense that you care, you can get more mileage from them. Usually before they are confronted, encouragement helps them to fully receive your information. These persons are steady and consistent. They have a tendency to be very industrious and diligent people.

Martha was a High S. Luke 10:38-42

C: This person has a tendency to be critical of self. They desire to know specifically *what can I do to improve and grow into a better person*. They prefer a slow, inch-by-inch approach to change. When sudden decisions are made for quick changes, this can be a very difficult situation for them to adjust to. Answer their questions in a patient and persistent manner.

Thomas and Luke were high Cs. Luke 1:1-4, Acts 1:1-2

We are to be intentional in our close encounters with each other in how we speak, lead, or communicate with each other, particularly if we work, live, or associate with them on a regular basis.

Knowing these four personalities will give you a clearer understanding to be more strategic and effective with others.

Which of the DISC areas mentioned do you believe right now closely aligns with who you are? Also, would someone approaching you from that perspective make you less defensive and more comfortable in resolving a matter or issue?

Chapter 9:
It's Not Always What You Think

Be careful with your words, because once they are said, they can only be forgiven, not forgotten

There is a humorous story of two women on a sunny afternoon who walked by a handsome man sitting on a park bench. One of them said, let me go over there and to talk to him. She went over to the park bench and sat down next to him. He calmly told her: I just got out of prison. I was in prison because I was convicted of killing three people. The first person, I had to choke her. The second person, I accidentally shot him. The third person was my wife, who I got into an argument with and stabbed to death. After listening to this frightening information, she slowly got up and went back to her girlfriend, who was waiting to hear the exciting news about this handsome man. She told her girlfriend that he was single and he said he was interested in her.

Moral of the story: Be careful who you listen to, because situations and people are not always who and what they look like. Some people, whatever their motivation, will draw you into their mess and stress.

The question remains, how can we be careful that we are not over-reaching or making quick judgments that will later reflect poorly on us?

Be Careful in Your Dealings with Them

***Don't throw out* what you don't want thrown back at you.**
Some people could say mind your own business. In other words, don't let your food get cold worrying about what's on my plate. Notice the consequences. We all fall victim to the truth: "You will reap what you sow." Conversely, the other reality is that what we refuse to deal with, will eventually deal with us.

Why? Proverbs 26:27
"Whoever digs a pit will fall into it; if someone rolls a stone, it will roll back on them."

You may say, what is the difference between judging and observation?
- Judging - bringing accusations and condemnation on someone or something without the sunshine of clarity or full understanding, and assuming the worst about a situation.
- Observation - describing, and at the same time not injecting your personal opinion or judgment into, what you see, and not demonizing, condemning or demoralizing the other person or

situation. In other words, until we get enough information, we should keep a gracious open mind.

I have learned that there are three principles concerning judging one another:

1. Be careful and give it time - 1 Corinthians 4.5

"Therefore judge nothing before the appointed time; wait until the Lord comes. He will bring to light what is hidden in darkness and will expose the motives of the heart. At that time each will receive their praise from God."

2. It's not always what it looks like.

A husband goes to the jewelry store with one of his female coworkers to assist him in purchasing a diamond bracelet for his wife for their anniversary. His wife just happens to be in the same area, walks by the jewelry store, and notices through the glass window her husband in the store with another woman, placing this bracelet on the wrist of his coworker to see how it fits. His wife is infuriated by what she sees. What do you think their dinner together later that night was like? Remember, it's not always what it looks like.

3. Don't let people stress you into their mess.

You may face the possibility of turning into a hater and forming a heart of jealously. We saw this in the behavior of King Saul toward young David. The people chanted that Saul has killed his hundreds, but David has killed his thousands. When King

Saul heard this, he judged David as a threat. The Bible tells us Saul kept a jealous eye on David. The Bible also tells us at that moment, an evil spirit came forcefully upon Saul. Be careful what and who you open your soul up to. Saul was his friend; now, because of the voices of other people, David was a threat to him.

In effect, Saul became a "frenemy". This is someone who is close to us, either by proximity or by a common relationship through a particular task, but strangely, someone you don't trust. If you are not careful, you will find yourself in one or more of the four frenemy situations listed here.

- Hater Friend - complains and is negative about everything
- Envious Friend - someone who won't celebrate your dreams
- Flaky Friend - always backs out of commitments but expects you to keep your commitments.
- Fearful Friend - reminding you what you can't do. You may hear the phrase "If I were you."

We Need a Mirror, Not a Window

Saints, be careful of people drawing you in to be stressed in their mess. Jesus said, "judge not, lest you be judged." I don't know about you; I can't afford to throw out what I don't want thrown back at me. We need a *mirror* to *reflect* on ourselves and our motives, and not a *window* to look out and *reject and readily condemn others*. I personally know that I live on the grace and mercies of God. I am not better or less than anyone else. I can't afford to get caught up being a fruit inspector. I have

Flawed Pots

enough bruises and challenges in my own life, to be looking at and demeaning anyone else's bruised fruit. If God was to judge me on everything I have done, I would have suffered in ways greater than the comfort I am now experiencing. But we have a Jesus who knows what it's like to be misunderstood. He was lied to. He was talked about, beaten and rejected. In fact, the cross at Calvary was the price Jesus paid for being misunderstood. It's not always what it looks like. How we see and understand each other is critical to creating resolutions in our often-conflicted relationships.

Let's look at Matthew 7:3-5

Why then, do you look at the speck in your brother's eye, and pay no attention to the log in your own eye? How dare you say to your brother, please let me take the speck out of your eye, when you have a log in your own eye? You hypocrite, first take the log out of your own eye, and then you will be able to see clearly to take the speck out of your brothers eye.

Look in the mirror before you look out the window

In other words, the other person's issues are really small compared to the personal issues you have (log in your own eye) first. Many of us need to reflect (take the log out) and ask: why does this person or situation tick me off? Then, you will be able to see clearly.

1. We can't always see what we can't see

Dr. Donald Davenport

I was driving one day and was ready to change lanes. I looked in the rear-view mirror, and then looked at the side-view mirror. Something in my spirit whispered and said take a second look, and actually look with your own eyes. There was a car hidden between the side-view mirror and the rear-view mirror. They call that area between a "blind spot." Just because I didn't see it, didn't mean it wasn't there. We all have a blind spot when it comes to understanding other people and their points of view.

Yes, there is a spiritual blind spot beam - even when we reflect in a mirror and see through a window. Jesus knew this irony, and that is why He said in verse 3: *why do you see the splinter in the other person's eye when there is this plank in your eye?*

The Bible speaks about David, who now is King - but he also had blind spot. You may be familiar with the story. David had Bathsheba's husband Uriah killed. David did it by setting Uriah up to be killed, placing him in battle on the front lines.

Nathan, the priest and prophet, confronted David and shared with him the story of someone stealing another owner's sheep. David was infuriated by the story and wanted to destroy this man who stole the sheep. Nathan said: You are that man. Now, the question for us is, why couldn't David see himself in this story? He was essentially blinded by the same sin.

Remember, Saul was blinded by jealousy, and David was blinded by his own guilt and shame.

Flawed Pots

These men loved God, but lived with the common realities of their flawed lives and choices that led to their eventual downfall and shame.

2. You might miss what God has for you

Be careful of creating a blind spot of **projecting** your issues to other people. There is a common saying that goes like this: "Don't judge a book by looking at the cover." For example, single women and men often make judgements about the opposite sex by merely looking at them and determining that they are not their type. You may find out that you may be missing a blessing of the one person God has for you. All because we judged or made conclusions about this person because they remind you, for example, of your former or past failed relationships.

They may not be who you want - but they may be who you need. You ought to say: Lord, you show me. Remove the beam from me. Why am I upset or turned off by this person? Is this person before me being difficult, or am I the one who is being difficult? Is this attitude or thought against God's word? Is this a threat to my home, group, or who I am as a person?

3. You don't know what people are going through

A well-known preacher, struggling within his church ministry, said he was building a $45 million church building. At the same time, his mother had a stroke. It soon led his mother to suffer dementia. He hurries home each Sunday morning, after preaching for everybody else to be encouraged, to deal with the struggle of caring for his own mother, who had no memory of him. This pastor had to deal with the pain of others, and yet also has to deal with his own human personal drama. We never know.

Just a final reminder to be careful not to jump the gun in misunderstanding persons we may perceive as being difficult, because situations and things are not always what they look like or appear to be. We may find ourselves making mistakes that cannot be reversed.

The Faithful Dog and His Master

Once there lived a man in a village. His daughter unfortunately died soon after the birth of her child, and he was forced to raise his grandchild the best way he could. He loved this child very much. He also had a faithful dog that he trusted and that lived with him for many years. This dog was always eager to love, please, and serve his master.

One day, the baby had a high fever. The grandfather had to go to the nearby small town to bring medicine for the child. He left the baby sleeping in the cradle. His faithful dog was there to look after the child. The grandfather's intent was to come back as quickly as he could.

In the grandfather's absence, a wolf entered the house. After a short period of time, the old man returned home with the medicine. He entered the house, and the first thing he noticed was the paws and the mouth of his faithful dog were covered with blood. He thought that the dog had harmed and possibly killed his only grandchild. While the dog was licking his master's feet, the old man was filled with anger and a feeling of betrayal. In a fit of anger, he went and got his shotgun, and shot dead the pet that had served and loved him for many years.

When the old man went into the bedroom, he found the baby sleeping quietly and safely in the bed. He also noticed a wolf lying dead nearby. When the old man saw that his grandchild was alive but quietly sleeping, he was sad because he had mistakenly killed his faithful dog. He at once realized his mistake, that his faithful dog must have fought the wolf to keep it from harming the baby, but it was too late. He felt guilty, shameful, and regretted his behavior.

Moral of the story: Look before you leap to conclusions and judgments.

The challenge in the various relationships that we encounter on a daily basis is to realize that we all are God's children with faults, flaws, and weaknesses who seek to live out our best lives, often in difficult situations. As believers, we have been chosen to live out what the apostle Paul describes as a ministry of reconciliation, striving to be ambassadors of God's grace and truth with all of God's people. We do this because we are all, in essence, cracked or flawed pots, essentially seeking love and acceptance. Hopefully, as we continue to grow and learn in our walk with God, we will handle and embrace each other as our loving and gracious God sees us.

Conclusion
At the risk of being redundant, I want to emphasize this need to extend ourselves in tolerance in our

Christian community. Years ago, there were Christians who attached a large white button on their shirts for all to see. It had large, black capital acrostic letters printed on this button (PBPWMGINFWMY) which, when interpreted, stood for *Please Be Patient With Me, God Is Not Finished With Me Yet.* The reality is we are all in the slow crockpot process of maturity. Until then, daily place your heart toward God's light. Here is another illustration that will hopefully shed a little more light.

Place your heart toward the light
Often in ancient Jewish marketplaces, the sellers or vendors would display their pottery outside to be purchased for sale. However, the most unscrupulous venders would place their table away from the light of the sun and turn any pottery that was marred,flawed or cracked around, away from the initial sight of the prospective buyer. The wise buyer would be aware of the tricks of the seller, and take the pottery and hold it up to the light of the sun to reveal any potential flaw.

May each of us do the same. Let us all daily place our hearts up toward the light of God, so that His Son will reveal any spiritual flaws and cracks in order for His grace and mercy to heal us.

ADDENDUM

Behavioral Covenant - Sample

Mission - To create a healthier congregational culture that reflects God's purpose and will for the church, and to create preventative measures and a uniform process of spiritual support and encouragement in the body of Christ.

<u>The Goals of a Church Behavioral Covenant</u>

a. Having "holy conversations" where you can speak the truth in love, and not have "self-centered conversations" where you beat up on people who are not there and avoid speaking the truth to each other in love.

b. Creating a support system in the body that reinforces standards of behavior.

Colossians 3:13-16

Dr. Donald Davenport

1) *"Bear with each other and forgive one another if any of you has a grievance against someone. Forgive as the Lord forgave you. And over all these virtues put on love, which binds them all together in perfect unity. Let the peace of Christ rule in your hearts, since as members of one body you were called to peace. And be thankful. Let the message of Christ dwell among you richly as you teach and admonish one another with all wisdom through psalms, hymns, and songs from the Spirit, singing to God with gratitude in your heart.*

2 Timothy 4:2

2) "Preach the word; be prepared in season and out of season; correct, rebuke and encourage with great patience and careful instruction."

Why is this Covenant important?

a) Talking to and not about each other, and giving permission to ourselves to care for each other, is a biblical approach to provide integrity in the body.

b) The local church, the ecclesia, the people of God, and yes, even this ministry made up of flawed imperfect people serving a perfect and loving God.

Our Covenant to God

We promise to pray, alone and together, to thank God and to seek His help for our church, as we promise to listen to God's answer for us.

Sample: Our Covenant to Each Other

1. We promise to be a people who encourages and embraces our differences and similarities that do not violate clear biblical standards and principles.
2. We promise, in times of ungodly behavior by individuals, to admonish and hold them accountable in the spirit of Christ that is in accordance with Matthew 18:13-15
3. We will challenge and hold accountable all of our elected or selected leaders to be held to high moral and biblical standards and example of godliness
4. We will seek to correct and admonish each other in love when we see a brother or sister in a fault or ungodly behavior; we seek self-examination in the spirit of Galatians 6:1-2
5. We promise to create a culture of tolerance that affirms our Christian beliefs of God's Word of respect for each other and God's Word
6. We promise to listen with an open, nonjudgmental mind to the words and ideas of others in our church.
7. We promise to support and pray for our ministries, pastors, and staff, so their efforts can be most productive and so that they live a life above reproach.
8. We promise to discuss, debate, and disagree openly in meetings, expressing ourselves as clearly and honestly as possible, so that we seek to understand and not just be understood.
9. We promise to uphold biblical principles to embrace and support the final decisions of

Dr. Donald Davenport

our pastors and leaders, whether it reflects our personal views or not.
10. We promise that before we seek to personally correct and care for a, member, we must ask ourselves these five questions as we begin the first of a three-step biblical process for discipline and care presented in Matthew 18:15-17.

- *Have I sought God in prayer for His wisdom? Read Galatians 6:1-2*
- *Does the offense violate biblical boundaries? Read Galatians 5:16-26, 1 Corinthians 6:1-12*
- *Is this a flagrant act that is observed by and known by others in the church and community?*
- *Is this a continual action of sinful behavior?*
- *Is the congregation potentially at risk?*

BEHAVIORAL ZONES

Relationships in leadership are complex and an inexact science. Individuals in groups and ministries often interact in ways that can be helpful or harmful to each other. These behaviors often can determine the health and success of a group. The behavior grid below is more integrative than sequential and cannot be reduced to math or equations. When boundaries in relationships are violated, reactions happen. There are emotional boundaries such as: Responsibility (John 15:12) Respect (Mt.7:12) Freedom (Gal. 5:13-15) that are often crossed or violated.

When God in the Garden of Eden was seeking **reconciliation**, because the boundary of freedom was violated asked Adam and Eve about what they did. They choose to isolate or withdraw from God by blaming Him and each other. **Retaliations** also withdraws from personal relationships, but usually by anger over what was done to them because of some perceived **dominating** behavior. Retaliation and **isolation** both retreat or are reactive, but for different reasons. One seeks to harm others-the other harms themselves. The goal should be to honor each other's boundaries through intentional reconciliation and resolution through God's spiritual and biblical principles.

Until you change your thinking, you will always recycle your experiences

RECONCILIATION We can work this out	DOMINATION I am in control of this situation
Empowerment and ownership Gracious and merciful speech How can we understand each other Building a reconciled community Living in our truth: integrity, passion, identity and adaptive **Am I operating in the capacity of love?** *Cooperation*	Subjugate others to self interest Listen to me Do as I say I need to be seen and heard **Am I operating out of some fear?** *Control*
RETALIATION I won't let you get away with this	ISOLATION I have got to get away
Withdrawal to harm others The relationship between Jacob and Esau Repaying Evil **Who does vengeance really belong to?** *Revenge*	*Walls; rejection, fear, shame and blame* Withdrawal to harm self Fear that one's own needs are not met State of hopelessness to withdrawal I am leaving this situation I might get caught I feel ignored **How is this hurting me?** *Rejection*

Resolution
1. Admit your area in the behavioral zone above
2. Admit your selfishness in the relationship-what did I learn about myself and the other person
3. Begin acting out of love: 1 Corinthians 13
4. Thank God for the other person in the relationship: 1 Thessalonians 4

Sources and Works Cited

Introduction
Beyonce CD "Flaws and All"

Chapter 1
Colossians 3.17
Romans 12:18
Galatians 6:1-2 NIV
Proverbs 15.1
Proverbs 12.6
Proverbs.7.14
1Corinthians 15.33
1 Peter 2.8
Romans 12:18
2 Samuel 16.5-6
Proverbs 15:1
2 Samuel 16.11
Galatians 1:10 GNB)

Chapter 2: Gray Areas That Create Difficult People
Romans 14.1-14 NIV
Romans 12.18
1 Corinthians 10.25
Proverbs 26.27
Galatians 6.1-2
Face Book Post January 2019

Chapter 3: Elephants in the Room
Revelations 2.20,21 NIV

Chapter 4: The Challenges of a Jezebel Spirit
1 Kings 16.31
1 Kings 18.4
I Kings 18.38
Revelations 2.20
I Kings 21.1-15
I Kinga 21.17
1 Kings 21.23
2 Kings 9.34
Revelations 2.19-21
1 Kings 21.15-16 NLT
James Baldwin quote

Chapter 5: Fighting Righteously
Great Church Fights, p117 Leslie Flynn Abe Books 1976
Ephesians 4.3
Romans 14.19
1 Peter 3.11b
Nehemiah 5:1-19
Exodus 22.25
Deuteronomy 23.19

Matthews 18:15
Mark 3.5
Proverbs 16.32
Luke 23.34
Acts 7,59-60
1 Samuel 25.2-3

Chapter 6
1 Samuel 15.1-12
The Angry Smile Workbook , Nicholas James Long, 2009

Chapter 7
Ephesians 4.15
Proverbs 15.1
Colossians 4.6
Matthew 18
Proverbs 11.14,24.6
1 Samuel 24.10
1 Samuel 8.7
Matthew 7.3-5
Proverbs 28.13
Romans 14.10-13
1 Corinthians 1.3-4
1 Corinthians 16.23-24
Matthew 5.44,45
Acts 15.37-40
Galatians 6.1-12
Isaiah 22.17-19

Chapter 8: Steps to Loving Unlovable People
DISC Method, William Moulton Marsten

Chapter 9: It's Not Always What You Think
Proverbs 26.27
1 Corinthians 4.5
Matthew 7.3-5

www.ingramcontent.com/pod-product-compliance
Lightning Source LLC
Chambersburg PA
CBHW030000050426
42451CB00006B/67